S. Hrg. 113–582

IRAN: STATUS OF THE P5+1 NEGOTIATIONS WITH IRAN

HEARING

BEFORE THE

COMMITTEE ON FOREIGN RELATIONS
UNITED STATES SENATE

ONE HUNDRED THIRTEENTH CONGRESS

SECOND SESSION

JULY 29, 2014

Printed for the use of the Committee on Foreign Relations

Available via the World Wide Web: http://www.gpo.gov/fdsys/

U.S. GOVERNMENT PUBLISHING OFFICE

WASHINGTON : 2015

93–521 PDF

For sale by the Superintendent of Documents, U.S. Government Publishing Office
Internet: bookstore.gpo.gov   Phone: toll free (866) 512–1800; DC area (202) 512–1800
Fax: (202) 512–2104   Mail: Stop IDCC, Washington, DC 20402–0001

(II)

CONTENTS

(III)

IRAN: STATUS OF THE P5+1 NEGOTIATIONS WITH IRAN

TUESDAY, JULY 29, 2014

U.S. SENATE,
COMMITTEE ON FOREIGN RELATIONS,
Washington, DC.

The committee met, pursuant to notice, at 10:01 a.m., in room SD–419, Dirksen Senate Office Building, Hon. Robert Menendez (chairman of the committee) presiding.

Present: Senators Menendez, Boxer, Cardin, Shaheen, Coons, Murphy, Kaine, Markey, Corker, Risch, Rubio, Johnson, Flake, McCain, and Paul.

OPENING STATEMENT OF HON. ROBERT MENENDEZ, U.S. SENATOR FROM NEW JERSEY

The CHAIRMAN. This hearing will come to order. We have two panels today to give us an overview of the status of the P5+1 talks, looking back at what we have learned over the last 6 months and looking ahead at what might change between now and November that ultimately gets us the type of deal we all hope for.

What I would like to hear from our witnesses, who have been across the table from the Iranians, given the underwhelming concessions achieved to date, is what you have learned over the last 6 months that leads you to believe that we can reach a comprehensive deal in the next 4 months.

Now, I think everyone knows where I stand. I have been skeptical of the Iranians' sincerity from day one and I cannot say that I am any less skeptical today than I was 6 months ago. I do not believe Teheran has had a change of heart about its nuclear program. If it did, I would think that the whole militarization aspect of it would be part of something that still have to be negotiated, but would be up front. As a matter of fact, I think it should have been up front from the very beginning in order so that we could define truly the nature of these negotiations in a way that the world would not just suspect that Iran was pursuing nuclear weapons, but would know it.

I do believe that the Iranians want relief from sanctions and that is why they are at the table. I also believe we have leverage in this negotiation and that we should use it to get a good deal, and if not a good deal then no deal at all.

Now, on that I will say that I have joined with the administration many times and Secretary Sherman has on different occasions publicly and privately said that no deal is better than a bad deal. But lately I hear refrains from the administration: But if no deal,

(1)

what? Which suggests that, in fact, if we have no deal there are those who suggest that that is a choice between getting some type of a deal or having to go to a military action. I reject that as a choice. I believe that there are significant interim steps in between that lead us far from that ultimate conclusion.

I also get concerned when I hear "If no deal, what?", because that implies that you have to get a deal at any cost. So I know that there are those in the disarmament community and in the editorial pages who suggest that those of us who want to really make sure that we get a good deal somehow have this penchant for wars. I find it particularly amusing as it relates to myself. I was one of the handful of people who voted against the war in Iraq, for example, at a time that it was overwhelmingly popular to vote for war.

But as someone who has followed this for 20 years from my days in the House of Representatives on the House Foreign Relations Committee to the present, I know that the Iranians have gotten us to a point that by defying the international community we now accept things that we would never have thought were acceptable— levels of enrichment; changing their facility, not closing their facility at Fordow; changing the nature of their plutonium reactor at Arak.

So they have succeeded in moving us well along the lines of what they ultimately wanted by defying the international community, including the present President of Iran, who has boasted about that while he was moving that program along he was able to keep the West from significantly sanctioning Iran.

So if past is prologue, I think my skepticism is well rooted.

Now, what I want to know is whether you believe an extension will give us a good deal; a deal that alters Iran's nuclear heading, postpones breakout, dismantles Iran's illicit nuclear infrastructure, puts us in place of a long-term inspection, verification, and monitoring regime, and calibrates sanctions relief to specific benchmarks, including a resolution of the possible military dimension of Iran's program.

Now, I want to be very clear. I am not looking for the State Department's talking points today. I want to hear from our panelists why they believe, based on their experience over the last 6 months, four additional months will make a difference. What the committee needs to hear now is what happened at the negotiating table that brought Iran closer to their view to a deal if only they had another 4 months.

Now, let me close by saying what I have always said: I support the administration's diplomatic efforts. I have always supported a bipartisan two-track policy of diplomacy and sanctions. At the same time, I have always believed that we should only relieve pressure on Iran in exchange for long-term verifiable concessions that will fundamentally dismantle Iran's nuclear program, and that any deal be structured in such a way that alarm bells will sound from Vienna to Washington, Moscow, and Beijing, should Iran restart its program any time in the next 20 or 30 years.

I also want to be clear today that I do not support another extension of negotiations. At that point Iran will have exhausted its opportunity to put real concessions on the table and I will be prepared to move forward with additional sanctions.

With that, let me recognize Senator Corker for his remarks.

OPENING STATEMENT OF HON. BOB CORKER, U.S. SENATOR FROM TENNESSEE

Senator CORKER. Thank you, Mr. Chairman. I want to say that I think those are excellent opening comments and I think there has been bipartisan concern about where Iran is. Actually, looking back over our notes, we look back at the hearing we had on October 2013, where I think Wendy and David both were here and we talked about the extraordinary effort internationally that had been put in place to get Iran where they were when these negotiations began.

I think the statement you mentioned—and hopefully this will play out in this way—but Iran's compliance with all U.N. Security Council resolutions would be the ultimate test as to whether they really were willing to deal with us in the appropriate way.

I think all of us wish you well and all of us—I do not know of a soul here that does not want to see this resolved in a diplomatic way. I know we have had numbers of briefings, classified, some unclassified, and I will say in fairness the chairman is right. I mean, in each case on the important issues we feel the goalposts move.

In March, of course, the issue of enrichment was basically agreed to. It is going to be very difficult, I think, to walk that back. But then on so many issues that are related and tied to this, we see the goalposts again continue to move. I know that David's testimony today has done a good job, I think, with sanctions. He is going to talk about the relief that Iran is getting during this next 4-month extension.

But I think all of us are concerned that the—rightly so, and I think you are concerned, too—that the international community, having come together to put pressure on Iran the way that we have, is dissipating and will be very difficult to bring back together if we end up in the wrong place here.

So I will close. I think that the chairman's comments speak well for most of the committee, candidly. I will just close by saying this. I hope that today you will publicly commit that there will be absolutely no more extensions, none; no matter where we are at the end of this 4-month period, there will not be additional extensions.

We will either come to a final agreement or not, because I think people are very, very concerned about what happens if we have a series of rolling interim agreements, if you will.

Secondly, I hope you will commit, as John Kerry has said, that there needs to be congressional buy-in. I hope you will agree to some format that gives Congress the ability to weigh in on this final deal. I know everybody says these sanctions cannot be waived without Congress. Well, they can. They can be waived without Congress weighing in.

I actually believe that acknowledging Congress playing a role in one of the biggest issues that this administration is going to deal with relative to reaching agreement on nuclear issues—I think that Congress can be an important and valuable backstop to the administration as they negotiate this, because I know that Congress has sent out very, very strong signals as to what they believe, what we believe, would be an acceptable arrangement.

So thank you for being here. I appreciate your service to our country. I appreciate the updates that we received by phone and in person. Again, all of us want to see success, but are very concerned about where we are at this moment.

The CHAIRMAN. Thank you, Senator Corker.

For the record, your full statements will be included in the record, without objection. We would ask you to summarize them in about 5 minutes or so, so we can enter into a dialogue with you. With that, Madam Secretary, you are recognized.

STATEMENT OF HON. WENDY SHERMAN, UNDER SECRETARY FOR POLITICAL AFFAIRS, U.S. DEPARTMENT OF STATE, WASHINGTON, DC

Ms. SHERMAN. Good morning and thank you, Chairman Menendez and Ranking Member Corker and distinguished members of the committee. I am pleased to be here along with Under Secretary Cohen to discuss the status of negotiations related to Iran's nuclear program. As you say, you have my written statement, so I will summarize its key points.

Mr. Chairman and members, our goal is to prevent Iran from obtaining a nuclear weapon. The diplomatic process in which we are currently engaged was designed to achieve that goal peacefully and durably. We have a basic metric for a good agreement: one that cuts off all of Iran's potential paths to a nuclear weapon—the plutonium path with the current Arak reactor, the path through the underground facility at Fordow, the path through swift breakout at the Natanz enrichment plant, and the path that would occur in secret, which we will deal with through intrusive measures.

And we will tie our sanctions relief to Iran's performance, only providing relief to Iran after it has taken verifiable steps as part of a comprehensive agreement and maintain the capacity to tighten the pressure if Iran fails to comply.

I cannot tell you today that our diplomacy will succeed because I am not sure that it will. I can tell you that in the past 6 months we have made significant and steady progress. We have exchanged ideas, narrowed gaps on key issues, and identified areas where more hard work is required.

For instance, we have had productive discussions about how to reduce the dangers posed by the facilities at Arak and Fordow, about the protocols necessary for transparency, and about the disposition of Iran's stockpiles of enriched uranium. No issues have been neglected. None have been finally decided because nothing is agreed until everything is agreed. And on some we still have substantial differences, including the question of enrichment capacity.

As you know, Mr. Chairman, there is a limit to how detailed I can be in this open session and still preserve the leverage we need in support of the goal we seek. However, the bottom line is that, although serious obstacles do remain, we are moving in the right direction.

For that reason, roughly 2 weeks ago the parties to the negotiation agreed to extend our deliberations for 4 additional months. We agreed to this extension because we had seen significant progress in the negotiating room and because we can see a path forward, however difficult, to get to a comprehensive plan of action. We will use this time to continue working toward that comprehensive plan for ensuring that Iran does not obtain a nuclear weapon and that its program is exclusively peaceful.

I note that a year ago Iran's nuclear program was growing and becoming more dangerous with each passing day. That is no longer the case. Last November, as a first step in this negotiation, we reached consensus on a Joint Plan of Action. In return for limited and targeted sanctions relief, Iran agreed to freeze and even roll back key elements of its nuclear activities. In fact, the JPOA has temporarily blocked each of the paths Iran would need to go down to build a nuclear weapon.

Many observers openly doubted whether Iran would keep its commitments under the Joint Plan. But according to the IAEA, Iran has done what it promised to do during these past 6 months. The result is a nuclear program that is more constrained, more transparent and better understood than it was a year ago, a program that has been frozen for the first time in almost a decade.

Meanwhile, as Under Secretary Cohen will make clear, sanctions relief for Iran will remain limited to amounts that will do little, if anything, to heal Iran's deep-seated economic problems.

Over the next 4 months, the valuable safeguards that freeze Iran's nuclear program will remain in place as we strive to negotiate a comprehensive and longer term plan. I will be blunt and say that we will never rely on words alone when it comes to Iran. We have, and we will insist, that commitments be monitored and verified and that the terms of access and inspection be thoroughly spelled out.

Our goal is to structure an agreement that would make any attempt to break out of such an agreement so visible and so time-consuming that Iran would either be deterred from trying or stopped before it could succeed.

Speaking more generally, I want to emphasize that engagement on one issue does not require and will not lead to silence on others. The United States will not hesitate to express its view and to put pressure on Iran when it is warranted, whether in relation to the government's abysmal human rights record, its support for terrorism, its outright hostility toward Israel, or its detention of political prisoners, journalists, and American citizens.

Mr. Chairman and members of the committee, on this issue we are united in our goals. We are determined that Iran not obtain a nuclear weapon. It is only because of the leverage created by the executive and legislative branches of this government, by our allies and partners, and by the U.N. Security Council that Iran has come to the negotiating table in what we believe to be a serious way.

But we all know that sanctions are a means, not an end. We are now in the process of determining whether the end we seek can be achieved through a diplomatic process. That effort is worthwhile because a positive outcome would be preferable to any alternative. A comprehensive agreement would ease anxiety and enhance stability throughout the Middle East. It would reduce the likelihood of a regional nuclear arms race. It would eliminate the potential threat of nuclear blackmail. It would contribute to the security of Israel and to our partners throughout the region and it would make our own citizens safer.

Between now and the end of November we will continue our pursuit of these welcome ends, and it is with those high purposes in mind that I respectfully thank you and ask you again for your support. I thank you for the opportunity to be here. I will be pleased to respond to every question and be as specific and detailed as I possibly can, Mr. Chairman, in this open session.

Thank you.

[The prepared statement of Ms. Sherman follows:]

PREPARED STATEMENT OF WENDY SHERMAN

Good morning, Mr. Chairman, and Senators. I am pleased to be here and appreciate the opportunity to discuss with you the status of negotiations related to Iran's nuclear program.

Although there are many aspects of these deliberations that I will discuss today, the participants have agreed that, to give this process the best chance of success, we will refrain from speaking in public about the specific details of the negotiation. With that caveat, I will be as frank as possible. President Obama, Secretary Kerry, and the entire administration understand how vital a role Congress and this committee play in shaping U.S. policy toward Iran. We remain committed to regular consultations, to hearing from you, and to sharing ideas. We all have the same goal, which is to make the world a safer place both in the near future and for generations to come.

To that end, we seek to negotiate a comprehensive plan of action that, when implemented, will ensure that Iran cannot acquire a nuclear weapon and that Iran's nuclear program is exclusively peaceful. A good deal will be one that cuts off the various pathways Iran could take to obtain a nuclear weapon: a uranium pathway, through its activities at Natanz and Fordow; a plutonium pathway, through the Arak heavy water reactor; and a covert pathway. It will therefore need to include tight constraints and strict curbs on Iran's program, and enhanced monitoring and transparency measures to ensure that any attempt to break out will detected as quickly as possible.

In Vienna, 2 weeks ago, we decided to continue our work toward our goal by extending the terms of the previously negotiated Joint Plan of Action for 4 more months—until November 24. I will have more to say about that decision in a minute, but first let me review how we arrived at this juncture.

RALLYING THE INTERNATIONAL COMMUNITY

In 1968, Iran signed the Nuclear Non-Proliferation Treaty, which required it to allow International Atomic Energy Agency (IAEA) inspections and to develop nuclear power only for peaceful purposes. However, over the past 20 years, it became apparent that Iran's Government had engaged in a variety of undeclared nuclear activities. As detailed in numerous IAEA reports, these activities covered the full spectrum of the nuclear fuel cycle and suggested an intent that was far from peaceful. Iran also built a secret enrichment facility at Fordow, and in Arak, a heavy water reactor ideal for producing weapons-grade plutonium. Meanwhile, Iran was conducting research of a type that could facilitate the eventual construction of a bomb. These actions placed Iran in clear violation of its international nonproliferation obligations.

In 2009, when President Obama took office, he indicated America's willingness to engage directly with Iran to find a diplomatic solution, but Iran failed to respond positively, thus demonstrating clearly that the obstacle to a comprehensive resolution was in Tehran, not in Washington. Working together, the administration and Congress then constructed a much tougher bilateral and multilateral sanctions regime, even as we continued to offer Iran a diplomatic pathway to resolve our concerns about its nuclear program. The international community, having witnessed our decision to give diplomacy a chance, was increasingly supportive, and their efforts to comply with—and amplify—our sanctions have proved crucial in ramping up the pressure on Iran.

In June 2010, the Security Council approved stricter curbs on Iran's nuclear and shipping activities and barred Tehran from purchasing heavy weapons such as attack helicopters and missiles. In July of that year, the European Union (EU) prohibited joint ventures with Iran's petroleum sector and banned the sale of equipment used in natural gas production. In subsequent months, the EU tightened sanctions on banking, energy, and trade; outlawed transactions involving Iran's financial institutions; and embargoed the purchase of Iranian oil.

These stiffer multilateral sanctions were complemented by additional bilateral measures—imposed by the United States and a number of other countries—that targeted Iran's economy in general and its financial and energy industries in particular. The cumulative weight of these restrictions contributed in Iran to more than halving oil exports, rising inflation, a sharp decline in the value of the local currency, and higher unemployment.

Sanctions, however, are a means, not an end. The key question was what impact they would have on Iran's decisionmakers and whether they would choose to engage.

THE JOINT PLAN OF ACTION

In June 2013, Hassan Rouhani was elected President of the Islamic Republic with a popular mandate to fix the economy, a goal that will only be fully achievable if nuclear-related sanctions are lifted. Last September, a telephone conversation between Presidents Obama and Rouhani—spurred in part by earlier and direct diplomatic contacts at a lower level—set the stage for a restart of formal negotiations between Iran and the P5+1.

On November 24, 2013, after several rounds of intensive negotiations with Iran, we reached consensus on a Joint Plan of Action (JPOA), a mutual set of commitments that halted the advance and even rolled back parts of Iran's nuclear program. The implementation of the JPOA started in January and was originally scheduled to last 6 months. In that time, Tehran pledged to cap its stockpile of low-enriched uranium. It agreed to stop enriching uranium to 20 percent and to convert or dilute its stockpile of uranium that had already been enriched to that level. It promised not to fuel or install remaining components at the research reactor in Arak. It consented to increase its transparency by providing additional information and managed access to key sites by the IAEA. And it allowed inspectors to have daily access at the Natanz enrichment facility and the underground plant at Fordow. In these past 6 months, the IAEA has verified that Iran has complied with its commitments; it has done what it promised to do. In addition, the JPOA has provided time and space to negotiate a more comprehensive, long-term solution by keeping Iran's program from making more progress during that period.

VIENNA

Meanwhile, from January to July, the negotiating teams were hard at work in search of a durable and comprehensive settlement. Based primarily in Vienna, our discussions on all issues were serious and exhaustive. Our experts spent hundreds of hours engaged in dialogue about the technical details. We made tangible progress in key areas, including Fordow, Arak, and IAEA access. However, critical gaps still exist on these and a number of other important elements—including the pivotal issue of uranium enrichment capacity—that must be part of a comprehensive plan.

Under the current 4-month extension, the commitments under the JPOA will remain in effect. And, in fact, Iran has agreed in the time ahead to substantially increase the pace at which it is turning its stockpile of 20 percent enriched uranium oxide into fuel plates, including 25 kilograms over the next 4 months. That will make it much harder for that material ever to be used for a weapon. Iran will also mix depleted uranium with its inventory of up to 2 percent enriched uranium. The result is essentially a dilution of approximately three metric tons of material to its natural state and a step further away from the kind of highly enriched uranium that could be employed in a nuclear weapon.

In return, the P5+1 and EU will continue to suspend the narrow group of sanctions that we committed to suspend when the JPOA was negotiated and will allow Iran access to $2.8 billion dollars of its restricted assets, the 4-month prorated amount of the JPOA.

To sum up, under the JPOA, instead of becoming more dangerous over time, Iran's nuclear activities have been more constrained, more closely inspected, and more transparent. This is the first true freeze in Iran's nuclear program in nearly a decade.

Meanwhile, sanctions relief for Iran will continue to be targeted and limited to amounts that will do little, if anything, to heal Iran's deep-seated economic ills. From the perspective of international investors, Iran will remain closed for business. The overall sanctions regime will still be in place. Iran will continue to be cut off from the global financial system. Iran's oil sector will still be negatively affected by sanctions, as will Iran's currency. All told, we have sanctioned nearly 680 Iranian individuals and entities under our Iran sanctions authorities. And as we have demonstrated in the past few months, and throughout the past half dozen years, the Obama administration will continue to enforce sanctions rigorously and thoroughly.

We will also not hesitate to put pressure on Iran when that is warranted—whether in relation to the government's abysmal human rights record, its support for terrorism, its hostility toward Israel, or its detention of political prisoners. Engagement on one issue does not require—and will not lead to—silence on others. As I have noted repeatedly, we continue to press Iran to allow U.S. citizens Amir Hekmati and Saeed Abedini to return to their families as soon as possible, and to help us locate Robert Levinson, who went missing in Iran in 2007. We are also concerned about reports of Washington Post reporter Jason Rezaian's detention in Iran, along with two other U.S. citizens and the non-U.S. citizen spouse of one of the three. We call on the Iranian Government to immediately release Mr. Rezaian and the other three individuals as soon as possible.

Let me emphasize that the decision to extend the nuclear negotiations was taken only after careful thought. Each of the countries represented in Vienna, when weighing both sides of the issue, believed that it continues to be in our interest to identify a mutually acceptable framework. We did not want to allow impatience to prevent us from doing all we could to contribute to the future security and safety of the Middle East.

AMERICA'S COMMITMENT

I stress that these negotiations are fully in keeping with the administration's fundamental position. As President Obama has affirmed on numerous occasions, the United States will not allow Iran to obtain a nuclear weapon. That policy was in place prior to this negotiation; it is in place now; and it remains our solemn commitment. Because of the manner in which these negotiations have been structured and the pressure Iran continues to feel, Iran's leaders have a strong and ongoing incentive to reach a comprehensive resolution. If they cannot do that, then we will respond with greater pressure and with greater backing from the international community to do so because of our consistent and good faith efforts to resolve this situation diplomatically.

LOOKING AHEAD

Mr. Chairman, our purpose in entering these negotiations was to test Iran's unambiguously stated and often repeated commitment to an exclusively peaceful nuclear program. Accordingly, we have proposed a number of pathways whose elements would, in fact, give the world confidence that Iran's program is and will continue to be exactly that. As we have said from the beginning, this is a negotiation where every element of a resolution must come together in order for any aspect to work. It would not make sense to foreclose one route to a nuclear weapon and leave a second avenue untouched; nor would it be sensible—given Iran's history of illicit conduct—to equate Iran's promises with actions. We need far-reaching and tangible commitments on all fronts. That is the only way.

FINAL THOUGHTS

The next 4 months will allow us to determine whether a diplomatic solution is possible. As we have said many times, from the perspective of the United States, no deal is better than a bad deal. And yet, let us not forget that a comprehensive resolution, if we are able to arrive at one, will benefit people everywhere. It will ease anxiety and enhance security throughout the Middle East. It will reduce the likelihood of a nuclear arms race in the region. It will eliminate the potential threat of nuclear blackmail. It will contribute to the security of Israel, the Gulf States, and our partners throughout the region. Compared to any alternative, it will provide a more comprehensive, lasting, and peaceful solution to the concerns generated by Iran's nuclear activities.

Mr. Chairman and members of the committee, after our intense deliberations in Vienna these past 6 months, we believe strongly that it is worth taking additional time to pursue these very complicated and technical negotiations. We wouldn't have agreed to an extension if we did not have an honest expectation that we have a credible path forward; but we would have finished long ago if the task were simple. We still have work to do. We still have time to determine whether we can close the gap between what Iran has said it intends and what it is willing to do.

From the outset, these negotiations have been about a choice for Iran's leaders. Officials in Tehran can agree to the steps necessary to assure the world that their country's nuclear program will be exclusively peaceful, or they can squander a historic opportunity to end Iran's economic and diplomatic isolation and improve the lives of their people.

Meanwhile, all of our options remain, as does our determination to resolve one of the most pressing national security issues for America, for the region, and for the world.

In closing, I want to say to you on behalf of the entire administration that we welcome your thoughts, thank you for giving diplomacy a chance to succeed, respectfully solicit your support, and will be pleased to respond to any questions you might have.

The CHAIRMAN. Secretary Cohen.

STATEMENT OF HON. DAVID S. COHEN, UNDER SECRETARY FOR TERRORISM AND FINANCIAL INTELLIGENCE, U.S. DEPARTMENT OF TREASURY, WASHINGTON, DC

Mr. COHEN. Chairman Menendez, Ranking Member Corker, distinguished members of the committee, thank you for your invitation to appear before you today along with my colleague, Under Secretary Sherman, to discuss the extended Joint Plan of Action. I will focus my oral testimony this morning on our efforts to maintain intense pressure on Iran, to help achieve a successful outcome in the negotiations over its nuclear program, and the ever-mounting pressure that Iran will continue to face during the extended Joint Plan of Action period as the P5+1 seeks a comprehensive and long-term resolution to the international community's concerns over Iran's nuclear program.

When we announced the Joint Plan last November, we said that we did not expect the relief package in the JPOA to materially improve the Iranian economy, and it has not. The depths of Iran's economic distress, distress that resulted in large measure from the collaborative efforts of Congress, the administration, and our international partners, dwarfed the limited relief in the Joint Plan of Action.

So today as we start to implement the extended JPOA, Iran remains in a deep economic hole. The value of Iran's currency, the rial, has declined by about 7 percent since the JPOA was announced last November. Since 2011, Iran has lost about $120 billion in oil revenues. It lost $20 billion in revenues in the first 6 months of the JPOA and stands to lose an additional $15 billion in oil revenues during the next 4 months alone. Iran's economy today is 25 percent smaller than it would have been had it remained on its pre-2011 growth trajectory.

Now, when we entered into the JPOA some predicted that our sanctions regime would crumble, and some also argued that Iran's economy would rebound dramatically. Neither occurred. The fact is as we enter the 4-month extension of the Joint Plan of Action our sanctions regime remains robust and Iran's economy continues to struggle. And we remain confident that 4 months from now our sanctions will continue to bite and Iran's economy will remain under great stress.

The 3 to 4 billion dollars' worth of relief that the extended Joint Plan of Action may provide Iran pales in comparison to what Iran needs to dig itself out of its deep economic hole. We expect that firms will continue to shun Iran, as was the case during the first 6 months of the Joint Plan of Action. Firms have good reason to remain reluctant about doing business in Iran. The overwhelming majority of our sanctions remain in place. Iran continues to be cut off from the international financial system and is largely unable to attract foreign investments. Iran is still shut out of the United States, the world's largest and most vibrant economy, and precluded from transacting in the dollar. And there are a sweeping set of nearly 680 Iran-related sanctions designations, developed in concert with partners around the world, remains in place.

Throughout the JPOA period, we have also vigorously enforced our sanctions, recognizing the essential role that financial pressure played in the lead-up to, and now during, the Joint Plan of Action and how important maintaining that pressure will continue to be during this extended Joint Plan of Action period. Indeed, since the Joint Plan was negotiated we have imposed sanctions on more than 60 entities and individuals around the world for evading U.S. sanctions against Iran, aiding Iranian nuclear and missile proliferation, supporting terrorism, and for abusing human rights.

Throughout this short-term extension of the Joint Plan, I can assure you that we will continue to make certain through word and deed that banks, businesses, brokers, and others around the world understand that Iran is not open for business and Iran will not be open for business unless and until it assures the international community of the exclusively peaceful nature of its nuclear program.

While this 4-month extension will provide additional time and space for negotiations to proceed, it will not change the basic fact that Iran's sanctions-induced economic distress has not receded. And over the next 4 months my colleagues and I within Treasury and throughout the administration will continue to echo President Obama's clear message, namely that we will come down like a ton of bricks on those who seek to evade our sanctions. That will help provide our negotiators leverage as we explore the possibility of a comprehensive and long-term resolution to the international community's concerns over Iran's nuclear program.

I am happy to respond to any questions the committee may have.

[The prepared statement of Mr. Cohen follows:]

PREPARED STATEMENT OF DAVID S. COHEN

Chairman Menendez, Ranking Member Corker, and distinguished members of the committee, thank you for your invitation to appear before you at this important time to discuss our implementation of the extended Joint Plan of Action (JPOA).

I will focus my testimony today on our efforts to continue to maintain pressure on Iran in order to achieve a successful outcome in the negotiations over its nuclear program. I will also provide an overview of the limited, temporary, and reversible relief in the extended JPOA. And, finally, I will discuss the ever-mounting pressure that Iran will continue to face as the P5+1 seeks a comprehensive and long-term resolution to the international community's concerns over Iran's nuclear program.

THE STATE OF THE IRANIAN ECONOMY

When we announced the JPOA last year, we said that we did not expect the relief package in the JPOA to materially improve the Iranian economy. And it has not. The depths of Iran's economic distress—distress that resulted in large measure from the collaborative efforts of Congress, the administration, and our international partners—dwarfed the limited relief in the JPOA. And so today, as we start to implement the short-term extension of the JPOA, Iran remains in a deep economic hole.

It is useful to focus on three key indicators of Iran's economy, the rial (Iran's currency), its revenues, and its reserves. Judging by these three measures, the Iranian economy is doing worse today than it was at the outset of the JPOA.

• Rial: Iran's currency, the rial, has depreciated by about 50 percent since January 2012 and has declined by about 7 percent since the JPOA was announced last November. Iran's central bank governor earlier this year bemoaned the fluctuations in the value of the rial in light of persistent costs and delays in obtaining hard currency and the limited tools available to intervene effectively in the currency market. In this regard, I would note that it remains sanctionable to provide U.S. dollar banknotes to the Iranian Government.

- Revenue: The cumulative impact of our sanctions since 2011 has caused Iran to lose about $120 billion in oil revenues—the key driver of Iran's economic growth. Iran will forgo an additional $15 billion in oil revenues during the next 4 months alone as the sustained impact of our oil sanctions, which took effect in early 2012, continue to exact their toll on Iranian earnings. Moreover, Iran will only be able to use a small fraction of the revenue it earns from crude oil sales during the extended JPOA period, because its oil revenue continues to go into overseas accounts restricted by our sanctions.
- Reserves: And the vast majority of Iran's approximately $100 billion in foreign reserves remain inaccessible or restricted by sanctions. This money can only be used for permissible bilateral trade between oil-importing countries and Iran and for humanitarian trade.

Iran's economy is 25 percent smaller today than it would have been had it remained on its pre-2011 growth trajectory; it will not recover those losses for years to come. Meanwhile, Iran's annual inflation rate, at about 26 percent, is likely to remain high, and is one of the highest in the world. Unemployment also remains high, and Iran is cut off from the foreign investment that it needs to promote job growth and infrastructure development.

At the time we entered into the JPOA, some made dire predictions that our sanctions regime would crumble, and that Iran's economy would rebound dramatically. It is now clear, that did not happen. To the contrary, Iran's experience under the JPOA has reinforced its knowledge that real economic relief can come only if it obtains comprehensive sanctions relief, and that can only come about if it is prepared to enter into a comprehensive plan of action that ensures that Iran cannot acquire a nuclear weapon and that its nuclear program is exclusively peaceful.

SANCTIONS RELIEF IN THE EXTENDED JPOA

The P5+1 has committed in the JPOA extension period to continue the limited, temporary, and reversible sanctions relief of the JPOA, and to authorize the release to Iran of a small fraction of its restricted overseas assets in return for Iran's commitment to continue to abide by the conditions on its nuclear program as set out in the JPOA, and to take a number of additional steps to constrain its nuclear program.

Over the 4-month period of the extended JPOA, and provided that it satisfies its commitments under the extension, Iran will be allowed to access, in tranches, $2.8 billion worth of restricted funds. This amount is the 4-month prorated amount of funds made available under the original JPOA.

Other aspects of the JPOA sanctions relief also will remain in effect for the next 4 months, including sanctions related to Iran's petrochemical exports, its crude oil exports to current purchasers at current average levels, its automotive sector, the purchase or sale of gold or precious metals, the licensing of safety-related repairs and inspection for certain airlines in Iran's civil aviation industry, and the facilitation of a financial channel for humanitarian trade, tuition payments, U.N. payments, and medical expenses incurred abroad.

Altogether, we value the sanctions relief in the JPOA extension at about $3 to $4 billion. This is comprised of the $2.8 billion worth of restricted funds that Iran will be permitted to access plus the value that we assess the other elements of the sanctions relief are worth.

EXTENDED RELIEF IN CONTEXT

We do not expect this minimal relief to alter the underlying negative fundamentals of Iran's troubled economy. We are confident in this assessment for the same reasons that we were confident in December that the JPOA would not undermine our sanctions regime: Iran is in a deep economic hole and we will continue to enforce our sanctions to send a clear message that now is not the time for businesses to re-enter Iran.

The value of this limited relief pales in comparison to the aggregate macroeconomic effects of our sanctions to date and Iran's revenue losses, both of which will continue to accumulate during the next 4 months. Even with the diminished value of Iran's gross domestic product—valued at about $360 billion today using the open market exchange rate—the $3 to $4 billion or so in relief over the next 4 months pales in comparison.

In short, Iran's economy will remain under great stress. Remaining sanctions and their substantial structural problems will undercut key industries and contribute to persistent budget deficits and sustained high unemployment. Moreover, until a comprehensive solution is reached, we anticipate that most foreign firms will decline to re-enter Iran, as was the case during the first 6 months of the JPOA.

THE INTERNATIONAL SANCTIONS REGIME REMAINS ROBUST

Firms have good reason to remain reluctant about doing business in Iran. The overwhelming majority of our sanctions remain in place, and we firmly intend to continue enforcing our sanctions vigorously.

Iran continues to be cut off from the international financial system with its most significant banks subject to sanctions, including its central bank. All the Iranian banks designated by the EU remain cut off from specialized financial messaging services, denying them access to critical networks connecting the rest of the international financial sector. And the fact remains that any foreign bank that transacts with any designated Iranian bank can lose its access to the U.S. financial system.

Investment and support to Iran's oil and petrochemical sectors also is still subject to sanctions. And there are severe restrictions on providing technical goods and services to the Iranian energy sector.

Broad limitations on U.S. trade with Iran remain in place, meaning that Iran continues to be shut out of the world's largest and most vibrant economy and precluded from transacting in the dollar.

Our sweeping set of designated Iran-related actors—developed in concert with partners around the world, including in the EU, Canada, Australia, Japan, South Korea, and Singapore—remains in place. We have used our Iran-related authorities to sanction nearly 680 persons, a number that is complemented by the hundreds of Iranian individuals and entities against which our partners have also taken action. This multilateral effort to target those involved in Iran's illicit conduct remains the cornerstone of the unprecedented sanctions regime that we have built in recent years.

Finally, we remain vigilant in our efforts to counter Iran's support for terrorism, its abuse of human rights, and its destabilizing activities in the region. We are committed to maintaining those sanctions and have an active diplomatic campaign aimed at persuading other jurisdictions and financial institutions to cut them off as well. Nothing in the JPOA, the extended JPOA, or in a comprehensive deal that may come, will affect our efforts to address Iran's malign activities in these areas.

VIGOROUS ENFORCEMENT OF EXISTING SANCTIONS

Throughout the JPOA, we have demonstrated vigorous sanctions enforcement, recognizing the essential role that financial pressure played in the lead-up to, and now during, the JPOA, and how important maintaining that pressure will continue to be during this extended JPOA period. We are determined to continue to respond to Iran's evasion efforts, wherever they may occur.

Since the JPOA was negotiated, we have imposed sanctions on more than 60 entities and individuals around the world for evading U.S. sanctions against Iran, aiding Iranian nuclear and missile proliferation, supporting terrorism, and for carrying out human rights abuses. This amounts to nearly 10 percent of all of our Iran-related designations and listings since we first took action against Iran's Atomic Energy Organization in 2005. We have also continued to enforce our sanctions against entities and individuals that violate Iran-related prohibitions, resulting in penalties and settlements for violations of the regulations enforced by the Office of Foreign Assets Control of more than $350 million during the past six months. We have been very clear to both our international partners and to Iran that these targeting and enforcement efforts will continue throughout the next 4 months of the JPOA extension.

In addition to our designations and enforcement actions during the JPOA, my colleagues and I have made clear to banks, businesses, and governments around the world that the sanctions relief provided to Iran is limited, temporary, and reversible, and that the overwhelming majority of our sanctions remain in place. The simple fact remains that foreign banks and companies still have to decide whether to do business with Iran, or with the United States. They can't do both. Nothing in this respect has changed.

These actions have sent a resounding message to the international business and financial communities: Iran is not open for business today, nor will it be until it ensures the international community of the exclusively peaceful nature of its nuclear program.

Throughout this short-term extension of the JPOA, I can assure you that we will continue to make certain that businesses and governments around the world understand this. I personally plan to travel to several countries in the coming weeks to meet with government and private sector counterparts to explain the continued limitations of the sanctions relief under the JPOA extension. And I know my colleagues within Treasury, at the State Department and elsewhere in the administration will do so as well. We will all echo President Obama's clear and firm message—namely, that we will come down ''like a ton of bricks'' on those who evade or otherwise facilitate the circumvention of our sanctions.

CONCLUSION

While this 4-month extension will provide additional time and space for the negotiations to proceed, it will not change the basic facts and numbers on the ground. The Iranian economy is in deep distress and an additional 4 months of limited sanctions relief will not change that. In the meantime, we will not let up one iota in our sanctions enforcement efforts, and we are prepared to take action against anyone, anywhere who violates, or attempts to violate, our sanctions.

The CHAIRMAN. Thank you both.

Before I get to the negotiation questions, I do have a question for you, Madam Secretary, about the detention of the Washington Post's correspondent in Teheran, Jason Reszayen, who I understand is a dual citizen, including a citizen of the United States, and his wife, who were arrested at their home last Tuesday. Since their arrests, no one has heard from them; and two U.S. citizens working as freelance photographers are also being held. To my knowledge, no charges have been brought and the detainees apparently have no access to legal counsel.

Can you tell me what we are doing in this regard?

Ms. SHERMAN. Yes. Thank you for raising this. It is of great concern to all of us, as is the continued detention of Amir Hekmati and Pastor Abedini and our concern about Robert Levinson, who has been missing for a very long time and we believe in Iran. We have, in fact, used our appropriate channels, principally the Swiss, to make known our concern about this apparent detention of American journalist and his wife and the additional photojournalists.

There is absolutely no reason for this to occur. I read with interest the Washington Post editorial, with which I entirely agree. We are a country that believes in press freedom. This is a reporter who has been reporting for some time, had been in Vienna with us, in fact during the negotiations, and we call on Iran to release all of these people, including Pastor Abedini, Amir Hekmati, and to help us in every way possible to return Robert Levinson home as well.

So thank you for raising this, and we will use every channel we have, Mr. Chairman, to continue to bring American citizens home.

The CHAIRMAN. Well, I appreciate that. More than raising it, I am concerned when U.S. citizens are detained by the Iranian Government. And I do not even understand the case of this reporter because, having read some of his articles, it seemed rather, I will not say favorable, but it certainly was balanced in his reporting.

So in the midst of negotiations, how is it that the Iranians detain U.S. citizens for what is from all apparent purposes nothing of any great consequence? I just, I do not get it. I do not get it, like I do not get the Ayatollah talking about 190,000 centrifuges at a time that we are trying to reduce the number of centrifuges. Even if he did not have it time specific, 190,000 centrifuges is beyond the pale of what we need.

So I hope we are vigorously going to pursue this with the Iranians and I hope they understand very clearly that actions like these undermine whatever negotiating posture they have at the table.

Let me ask you with reference to something that I think should have been a condition precedent. I think you and I have discussed this, but it certainly is a concern to me, which is the military, the possible military dimensions of Iran's program. I do not look at this as simply just to understand the past and say, you see. I look at it as a measurement for the future. If you do not know what Iran's military program was, you do not know to what point they progressed that will cause us concern that they are at a point maybe farther along than anyone suspects and a short jump toward being able to militarize their nuclear program for nuclear weapons.

And I think the world would have looked at these negotiations in a totally different way if that had been established up front. Now, my understanding from public reports—forget about private briefings—is that they are incredibly reticent to come clean on this issue. So what options are on the table for addressing the possible military dimensions of Iran's program, and will you insist—I do not think that this is giving away a negotiating posture—on access to persons, places, and documents for the IAEA to make this determination?

Ms. SHERMAN. Thank you very much, Mr. Chairman. We absolutely agree that possible military dimensions of Iran's program must be addressed as part of a comprehensive agreement. As you know, the International Atomic Energy Agency has a protocol under way to do that. It has been very difficult. Iran has been reluctant to come forward with the kind of information about people, places, and documents that——

The CHAIRMAN. Did they not recently say they are missing a deadline?

Ms. SHERMAN. They may indeed. There is an August 25 deadline coming up for some of the considerations. We have been in very close touch with Director General Amano because in our dealing with possible military dimensions in a comprehensive agreement we want to make sure we do not undermine the independence of the IAEA, but rather use the negotiations as leverage to get the compliance that is required, while at the same time ensuring that the IAEA can do its job and that we do not interfere with that in inappropriate ways, given their independence.

That said, I quite agree with you. If there is not access to what the IAEA needs to know about Iran's past, it is difficult to know that you will have compliance about Iran's future. How this will ultimately get resolved we have had quite a bit of discussion about. We have not reached a resolution on this issue. It is a very serious issue and must be resolved as part of a comprehensive negotiation. So I agree with you.

The CHAIRMAN. Let me ask you with reference to—assuming a good deal that we could all embrace—what is going to be critical after 20 years of deception is the monitoring and verification regime, which is why I have called for long-term inspections and a verification regime.

Some call that a suggestion of a deal-breaker. I do not quite get it. It seems to me that if you deceive for 20 years and you advance your program to a point that we are now accepting some level of enrichment, that we accept Fordow, which was supposed to be closed, that we were told that Arak was going to be dismantled either by them or by us, and now we are accepting all these things, that a long-term verification and management agreement is incredibly important, not a deal-breaker, but a deal-maker.

What monitoring and verification measures beyond the additional IAEA protocols are we seeking in a final agreement? And what types of verification measures are being considered to halt the procurement of key proliferation-sensitive goods as well?

Ms. SHERMAN. Thank you, Mr. Chairman. Transparency and monitoring is absolutely critical and core to any agreement. As I said, one of the pathways of greatest concern is, of course, covert action, and transparency and monitoring are the elements that help ensure that if there is a covert program one knows it in time to be able to take action and to stop it from happening in the first place.

In fact, in the Joint Plan of Action the fact that we can now have managed access to centrifuge production, to rotor production, to uranium in mines and mills gives our intelligence community and our experts the kinds of information that allow us to know whether something is being sent over to some other place and is not in the pipeline as is required to be inspected.

So in addition to modified Code 3.1 and the additional protocol, which are absolutely critical to a comprehensive agreement—and I believe Iran understands that—on each of the measures that will be agreed to we will decide whether, in fact, an additional element of transparency and monitoring is needed over the entire duration of this agreement. And the duration of this agreement, we agree with you, ought to be quite a long time, given how many years of concern have been raised by the international community.

So in some cases that will be access to sites. In some cases that will be other technical means of verification. But we will go element by element and make sure that there is, in fact, a specific monitoring and verification measure that matches up with that.

The CHAIRMAN. Let me ask you the specific question I asked before, and then I will turn to Senator Corker. Persons, places, and documents. Is that an unreasonable expectation in order to have the type of verification—both of the possible military dimensions or, prospectively—for 3 years before we found their underground facility. I do not know that while we agreed to something that allows them to do X, that they do not go ahead with their capacity somewhere else that we find 3 years later. But 3 years is going to be too late.

Ms. SHERMAN. We will do whatever the IAEA requires for verification. They have in the past required persons, places, and documents. I think they see the places and documents as the most important because they want to go and have direct access and look for themselves. The persons issue, as I think you know, is an issue for Iran, but it is one that is on the table and of great concern to us. Their concern is, to be very blunt and open about it, is if you name individuals that those individuals might find that their lives are quite short.

The CHAIRMAN. I think that there are ways for them to create access to individuals in their secure facilities that would guarantee that their lives would be extended.

Ms. SHERMAN. I agree, I agree.

The CHAIRMAN. Senator Corker.

Senator CORKER. Thank you, Mr. Chairman.

Ms. Sherman, is the administration in agreement that November 24 is the end of these negotiations, there will be no more extensions, that we either reach an agreement by that date or this negotiation is over?

Ms. SHERMAN. Senator, I have learned in negotiations that it is very difficult to say what will happen at the end of any given period of time. If you had asked me where we would be at the end of this 6 months that has just preceded, it would have been hard to predict that we are exactly where we are today. Our intent is absolutely to end this on November 24 in one direction or another, but what I can say to you is that we will consult Congress along the way.

I greatly appreciate that Congress has permitted classified briefings during active periods of negotiation to maintain whatever leverage we have. We will continue those classified conversations, and when November 24 comes whatever decision we make will be a joint one with the United States Congress.

Senator CORKER. And you understand the concerns people have——

Ms. SHERMAN. I absolutely do.

Senator CORKER [continuing]. About a series of rolling interim agreements?

Ms. SHERMAN. I do. And indeed, we made a very conscious decision not to go for a 6-month extension, which was possible under the JPOA, because we thought we would just get to month 5 before anything would happen. So we are concerned about talks for talks' sake as much as you are.

Senator CORKER. Then for the inspections regime, I think as the chairman alluded to and many people in these other settings have alluded to, if the inspection period is something short of 20 years or so we have really not done much, right? In other words, if we do not have a full inspection regime, if this agreement does not last for a long, long time, we really have dissipated all of our leverage for something that really does not matter.

What is the minimum length of time that is being discussed for an agreement of this type at present?

Ms. SHERMAN. We believe that the duration of this should be at least double digits and we believe that it should be for quite a long time. I am not going to put a specific number on the table today because that is a subject of very sensitive negotiations. But I am happy to discuss that with you in a classified setting.

Senator CORKER. Again, I think you understand the concerns——

Ms. SHERMAN. I do.

Senator CORKER [continuing]. That all of us have relative to something that is not very, very long term.

Ms. SHERMAN. And we share that.

Senator CORKER. Okay. Do you believe that they are agreeing to all their obligations in the JPOA?

Ms. SHERMAN. I do, and the IAEA has verified, which is even more important than my judgment.

Senator CORKER. So one of the areas where we have disputed this—and we have talked about it a little bit back and forth—is they agreed, there was an agreement that they were not going to export more than 1 million barrels per day. They are above that number, significantly above that number. I guess I would just ask the question, if they are significantly above the number they have agreed to, how are they in agreement with the JPOA? We believe they are at 1.4 million. I think you can verify that to be sure, I think. So how are they in agreement?

Ms. SHERMAN. Well, actually, Senator, I talked with our experts yesterday about this because I imagined that it would get asked today, and it is our assessment, having most of the data, though not having the last 20 days of July yet, that we will be within range of 1 to 1.1 million barrels per day, which is what, in fact, we had said would be the aggregate amount.

Now, some of the public data that is published includes two elements that are not part of that assessment. For those countries that are still allowed to import Iranian oil, though at the aggregate amount at which they were at at the time of the JPOA, that does not include condensates, and some of the public data includes condensates, which pushes up the number.

Secondly, some of the public data includes the oil that is headed to Syria and that pushes up the number, and indeed Iran gets no money directly from the oil they give to Syria, so they get no economic benefit to it. So if you take out the condensates——

Senator CORKER. I got it. If I could——

Ms. SHERMAN [continuing]. And take out Syria, we are at about 1 to 1.1.

Senator CORKER. I think that, just for what it is worth, the subtraction of condensates is a—I forgot what they called new math when I was a young man, but it is a very creative way of not counting all of their exports. We disagree strongly with those numbers.

But just think about what you just said. They are shipping oil to Syria. I will say it one more time: They are shipping oil to Syria instead of sending them money. They are working against us in that regard, and you do not count that as an export. I just find that to be ludicrous.

Ms. SHERMAN. Well, though we do have other sanctions through other channels for the export of that oil to Syria. So we do take enforcement action on that export.

Senator CORKER. Let me ask you this, two more questions. Secretary Kerry was in and said on April the 8th that the administration is obligated under law to come back to Congress for any relief of statutorily imposed sanctions on Iran, and any agreement with Iran will have to pass muster with Congress. Can you confirm that that is the case, and will you come to Congress prior to providing any relief associated with a comprehensive agreement? If not, why not?

Ms. SHERMAN. Senator, we believe strongly that any lifting of sanctions will require congressional legislative action.

Senator CORKER. Lifting, but you can waive. I want to get—— I heard you talk about the words, it is tough to resolve, a minute ago. I want you to clearly state to me: Will you, or will you not, come to Congress before lifting, whether it is a waive, a temporary waive, a skate down the road, whatever? No way will you lift any kind of relief on Iran, period, after this next agreement is reached or not reached, without coming to Congress?

Ms. SHERMAN. We cannot lift any sanctions without congressional action. We can, as you said, suspend or waive——

Senator CORKER. Right.

Ms. SHERMAN [continuing]. Under the current legislation. We will not do so without conversations with Congress. If you are asking, Senator, whether we are going to come to Congress for legislative action to affirm a comprehensive agreement, we believe, as other administrations do, that the executive branch has the authority to take such Executive action on this kind of a political understanding that might be reached with Iran. I cannot tell you whether we will or not.

Senator CORKER. I got that. I understand Article 2 of the Constitution. But I want to go back to what you are saying. You came and had a conversation with us, you and your representatives, and basically told us that you were extending the agreement. That is a conversation.

Ms. SHERMAN. Well—yes.

Senator CORKER. I just want to go back and I want you to clearly—waiving, suspending. You have told me you do not have to come back to Congress, and I would like to figure out a way that you do. I have been unsuccessful so far. But I want you to clearly state, on the waiving or suspending of any kind of sanctions, because you have the right to do that, you say you will have a conversation. Again, the conversations have been: This is what we are going to do. That is a very unsatisfactory place for us to be.

So you are telling me you cannot be any more clear than coming and having the same kind of conversations we have had in the past, where in essence you are telling us what you are going to do?

Ms. SHERMAN. Senator, the United States Congress and the United States Senate has oversight authority, has legislative authority. You are free to decide what action you think is appropriate for any executive branch decisions by any administration, and I understand those prerogatives quite clearly and I will commit to you that you will not be surprised by reading in the newspapers decisions or judgments that we have made, that we will keep you completely informed about what we are doing in these negotiations, as we have throughout these last 6 months.

Senator CORKER. Well, thank you. I know my time is up. I think the world understands that that is a zero commitment and it is not in keeping with what Secretary Kerry said on April the 8th. I know the goalposts keep moving and I think you can continue this hearing as evidence of why so many of us have the concerns we have.

Again, we wish you well.

The CHAIRMAN. Senator Cardin.

Senator CARDIN. Well, thank you, Mr. Chairman.

Let me thank both of our witnesses that are with us today for your continued service to our country. These are extremely challenging issues.

Going back to the start of these negotiations, I think we got off to a rough start between Congress and the administration. It caused, I think, more division than perhaps was in the best interest of this country. I want to thank you and acknowledge that I think, particularly in recent months, the cooperation between the administration and Congress has gotten much stronger. The openness of the briefings I think has been of much higher quality, and we thank you for that. The input from Congress has been pretty direct.

I think the administration has done a commendable job in keeping our negotiating partners together in unity, despite the challenges of international events. So I think we have made a lot of progress and I just want to acknowledge that.

I could not agree with you more that the objective is the visible ability, assuming we have an agreement, but the visible ability to determine if that agreement is not being adhered to. And as you point out, it would be very time-consuming to get back to the ability to produce a nuclear weapon. That is certainly the goal, and I think we all acknowledge that a bad agreement is worse than no agreement at all.

I think the language that we have been using has been pretty clear about that, the language that you have used, that if there is a failure here there will be tougher sanctions and tougher isolation, is absolutely accurate.

I just really want to follow up on one of Senator Corker's points, and that is November 24 would not be the end of this process. Because if I understand, if you are successful, Congress and the administration have to work together. The sanctions are not going to be removed all at once. There is going to be, I assume, a transition period that will require Congress and the administration to be on the same page on this.

So I just encourage you to use the same process that you have used during the last few months, which I think has been a much healthier process between the two branches of government that share the same objective. We have shared the same objective from the beginning. So I hope that you will continue to do that.

I want to just talk about the one part of your statement, Secretary Sherman, that you mentioned, and that is, we will also put pressure on Iran when it is warranted, whether it is in relationship to the government's abysmal human rights record, its support for terrorism, its hostility toward Israel, or its detention of political prisoners.

This has been, and is going to be, a lengthy process. Of course, we are focused on an extremely important priority for the United States and that is a nonnuclear Iran. But at the same time, Iran has other issues that are problematic to a relationship with the United States from the point of view of constructive relationships, and we have to use every tool that we can to deter them and to put a spotlight on the things that they are doing.

You then say you will not be silent. I assume silence means more than just words, that we will take actions in other areas, and nothing that we are doing in these negotiations would compromise our ability to speak out about these other issues that are critically important to the United States.

Ms. SHERMAN. I could not agree more, Senator. Where it comes to our sanctions on terrorism, our sanctions on human rights, they will continue in place. We have been quite clear with Iran that, although if we get to a comprehensive agreement there might be first suspension and then ultimately, after some period of time and after verification by the IAEA of a variety of benchmarks, ultimately perhaps lifting, that where it comes to our sanctions regarding terrorism, human rights, they will stay in place.

It is quite concerning, the actions that Iran takes in all of the arenas that you just mentioned—human rights, terrorism, fomenting instability. As the chairman said, who can imagine that detaining an American journalist helps these negotiations? In the past, I know it has been quite in the news of late, although Hamas creates many of its own rockets these days, a lot of the original supply of those rockets came from Iran. So the security of Israel is not only tied to this nuclear agreement, but it is also tied to their horrific rain of rockets that are coming down on Israel today.

So all of these areas we need to continue to have vigorous enforcement of our existing sanctions, take what other actions we can to mobilize the international community to condemn these actions, and to insist that they stop.

Senator CARDIN. I might point out—and again, at the end of the day, we must be together on this. It might be the preferred practice to use the waiver authority that you have rather than changing the underlying law in the event that we have to act quickly if there are problems in compliance, rather than having to wait for Congress to pass a new law and getting that to the administration.

So I just point out there are advantages to the tactics that are used at the end of the day. But I agree completely with Senator Corker and I think Secretary Kerry; it is critically important that we are together on this at the end of the day. I hope that will happen—and I know that you agree.

Secretary Cohen, I want to ask you one question about the challenges that you might be having today, considering that Europe and the United States are working for stronger sanctions against Russia. Russia is one of our negotiating partners in regards to Iran. Does that cause some challenges for you? I hope not. I hope that we are able to have more than one relationship at a time. This committee has been on record strongly supporting additional sanctions against Russia in regards to its actions with Ukraine. But is that affecting our ability to speak out as a unified voice in regards to Iran?

Mr. COHEN. Thank you for that question, Senator. The answer is not in the least. Our efforts to address Russia's destabilizing activities in Ukraine, its invasion of Ukrainian sovereignty and territorial integrity, have not been impeded one iota by the very important work that Under Secretary Sherman and the team have been undertaking in Vienna.

We have been pursuing a, I think, very powerful and calibrated strategy to impose pressure on Russia with respect to its activities in Crimea and now in eastern Ukraine. We have been working very closely with our counterparts in Europe and elsewhere to coordinate these actions. I think there have been press reports in the last

24 hours or so of additional sanctions yet to come. So I would stay tuned for that.

But we have not encountered any difficulty in terms of working with our partners or working ourselves to impose pressure on Russia in relation to the activities in Ukraine.

Senator CARDIN. Thank you.

Thank you, Mr. Chairman.

The CHAIRMAN. Senator Johnson.

Senator JOHNSON. Thank you, Mr. Chairman.

I have not had the years of experience with this issue as the chairman has, but the chairman was talking about moving the goalposts and I do have a lot of experience with negotiation. Certainly, when I sit down to negotiate I want to know and have a very clear understanding of what my goal is. I would also like to understand what the goal of the party is that I am negotiating with.

So my understanding is the goal of the world community, including the United States, as this all began was pretty well expressed in United Nations resolutions, correct? Ms. Sherman, can you state what that was?

Ms. SHERMAN. Yes, indeed, Senator. There have been more than one U.N. Security Council resolution regarding Iran's nuclear program, but it is to ensure that Iran cannot obtain a nuclear weapon and that its program is exclusively peaceful.

Senator JOHNSON. Was not the goal of the resolutions to end the enrichment program, to bar Iran from enriching uranium?

Ms. SHERMAN. Actually, what the language in the Security Council resolution is is that Iran should suspend enrichment, and in fact does not stop enrichment, bar enrichment, but urges that Iran suspend enrichment until there is assurance on behalf of the international community that its program is entirely peaceful; and in fact, even anticipates that they could resume if, in fact, they did provide that assurance.

That said, Senator, the administration position has been that the preference is that Iran not have an enrichment program, and that remains the case. In every negotiation I remind Iran that that is the case. They can get anything they need on the open market. They do not need an indigenous program. Nonetheless, at the end of this comprehensive agreement there is the potential for a very limited enrichment program for practical specific needs, under very intrusive mechanisms of monitoring and verification.

Senator JOHNSON. But as you said, there is no reason whatsoever to have enrichment, if your goal is only to have a peaceful, nonweaponized program, correct? There is none whatsoever. You can easily obtain these materials on the open market. You do not need to enrich to have a peaceful nuclear program.

Ms. SHERMAN. That is correct, and that is true of virtually every country in the world, and yet there are several countries that do have indigenous enrichment programs, some of our closest allies in fact.

Senator JOHNSON. Mr. Cohen, you made a pretty good case that, yes, we have relaxed sanctions, but the economy of Iran is still suffering quite severely. Again, I want to get back to the motivation then of Iran. They have suffered horribly in terms of economics and yet they will continue to enrich.

Would this not be very easy for them to just solve this problem by stopping enrichment?

Mr. COHEN. I think that is——

Senator JOHNSON. The answer is "yes." I am trying to get to a point here. I am trying to find out what is motivating Iran. We can sit here and talk about a peaceful nuclear program. That is not their aim, correct? Let us get it on the table. Let us show a little clarity here in terms of what Iran's objective is here.

Ms. SHERMAN. Senator, if we all were not concerned that Iran wanted to obtain a nuclear weapon, we would not be in these negotiations. They would not have been going on for some time. So of course we have concern. Up until 2003, the United States in a public intelligence estimate said indeed we believed Iran had been attempting to get a nuclear weapon. The intelligence community's assessment, which they can discuss further with you in private session, is that in fact after 2003 that particular program ended.

But of course we have that concern.

Senator JOHNSON. Here is my question. Why do we continue to pretend publicly that Iran will enter some agreement where it will be a peaceful nuclear program, that it will be exclusively peaceful? That will never happen. As long as they can enrich, they are doing it because they want to have that threat of being able to weaponize their nuclear program, correct?

So why not be honest? Why not be clear in terms of what Iran's motivations are? Why do we delude ourselves?

Ms. SHERMAN. I do not think we delude ourselves at all. As I said in my opening comments, what we are trying to do is to cut off every pathway to a nuclear weapon, to cut off their pathway through plutonium in their current Arak reactor, to cut off the pathway of highly enriched uranium through Natanz and Fordow, to cut off their pathway to a covert program by using intrusive monitoring and inspection.

So this is not about trust. This is not about being—some have illusions, some kind of illusion about them. This is about verification. This is about monitoring. This is about assurance to the international community. This is about inspections. So this is not about trust, Senator.

Senator JOHNSON. In a negotiation you want to maintain leverage. Now, I will stipulate, Secretary Cohen, that there is still pressure from a sanctions standpoint, but not as much. We certainly dissipated that negotiating leverage. But also just the fact that we implicitly agreed to their enrichment program also gave up an awful lot of negotiating leverage, did it not? Ms. Sherman?

Ms. SHERMAN. Senator, we made a judgment, the President of the United States made a judgment, that we could say that there was the possibility for a very limited enrichment program, mutually agreed, under strict limitations, with intrusive monitoring for a long period of time, to in fact deal with the international community's concerns about Iran's nuclear program.

As a result of that and that ability to have that element as a possibility on the table, brought about the Joint Plan of Action. That

Joint Plan of Action has ensured that in fact we have frozen the program at this time.

Senator JOHNSON. We have that in the testimony. I have heard that.

Let me ask my final question, and I will say "if." If this fails on November 24, what then?

Ms. SHERMAN. I think we will have very serious decisions to make. We will have consulted with you all along the way of these 4 months, a lot of that in closed session so that I can provide a great deal of detail to you, and we will decide what judgments we need to make.

There is no question, we have said if Iran will not reach a comprehensive agreement that cuts off all of their pathways to a nuclear weapon and that gives the international community the assurance we are looking for then we will step up right with you to additional sanctions and to considering all of the options which the President of the United States says remain on the table.

Senator JOHNSON. Would it not be smart right now to declare exactly what would happen, to create a little more negotiating leverage so maybe Iran gets a little more serious about this, as opposed to just talking about serious decisions or, even worse, maybe serious consequences?

Ms. SHERMAN. I can assure you that in our negotiations with Iran we are quite direct about what will happen and what could happen if we cannot reach a comprehensive agreement. They have no doubt about the United States resolve, absolutely none.

The CHAIRMAN. Senator Shaheen.

Senator JOHNSON. Thank you.

Senator SHAHEEN. Thank you, Mr. Chairman.

Thank you both for being here today and for all of your efforts to try and reach a comprehensive agreement with Iran.

Under Secretary Cohen, you talked a little bit in your opening statement about the economy in Iran. Shortly after the JPOA was announced, there were a number of business delegations from various countries, many of our allies, that went to Iran to, I assume, talk to them about prospects for business either in the interim or after a deal was reached. I wonder if you can talk about what we know about any of those discussions and whether we are still seeing the number of trade delegations continuing to go to Iran?

Mr. COHEN. Yes, Senator. We are not seeing as active a flow of trade delegations going to Iran as we did I think in the initial days after the Joint Plan of Action was reached. We were very clear at that time to our partners around the world and others that talk, if it moves into deals, consummated deals that cross our sanctions lines, that we will take action.

And we did, in fact, take a series of actions during the course of the Joint Plan of Action to make very clear that this was not just an idle threat, but we were very serious about continuing to enforce the vast sanction architecture that remains in place.

So we——

Senator SHAHEEN. Can you just——

Mr. COHEN. Sorry. Go ahead.

Senator SHAHEEN [continuing]. Delineate a couple of those in detail, so that we have some idea of exactly what was done?

Mr. COHEN. The sanctions? Sure. We took——

Senator SHAHEEN. Our response to the trade delegations.

Mr. COHEN. The response to the trade delegations was not specifically to—we had a number of outreach opportunities to governments to make clear to them that we did not think this was a great time to be engaging with Iran, even in conversations. Many of these trade delegations were from private businesses, not government-sponsored, and the way that we conveyed the message to those delegations was both through public messaging as well as through the sanctions designations that we took.

I do not think anyone was confused that we were going to sit back and allow sanctions violations to occur during the Joint Plan of Action without responding. We took action and I think that message was conveyed very clearly.

Senator SHAHEEN. If we do not reach a deal with Iran, to what extent do we expect our allies and other partners who have been involved in enforcing the sanctions regime to continue to be willing to comply with that effort?

Mr. COHEN. It is obviously difficult to predict the future in exactly how this will play out. But I do not have any doubt on two scores: One, if we do not reach a deal we will continue to enforce our sanctions very, very vigorously. The truth of the matter is, because of the significance of the United States economy, the significance of the United States financial system, the significance of our sanctions, that if there is not a deal the sanctions pressure on Iran will be maintained and intensified through actions of the United States alone.

But, that being said, I am also confident that we will be able to continue to rally to international community to the objective that people have subscribed to, which is that we are all working together to try to achieve resolution to the concerns with Iran's nuclear program. And there was complete buy-in to the notion that this dual-track approach of pressure on the one hand, but the opportunity to negotiate on the other, was the right way to proceed.

I think we will be able, if necessary, to regenerate that effort.

Senator SHAHEEN. I certainly agree that we are committed to seeing those sanctions stay in place. I just am concerned about where the rest of the international community is, particularly Europe and Turkey and some of our other allies.

Mr. COHEN. What I can say is that in the runup to the negotiations we I think were quite successful in persuading even somewhat reluctant allies to the wisdom of the approach, and if we are not able to reach an agreement with the Iranians I think the utility of a sanctions approach with the opportunity to negotiate will again be persuasive to our partners around the world, particularly as compared to the alternative of Iran developing a nuclear weapon.

So I think we will have work to do, but I am optimistic that we will be able, if necessary, to bring together the international community to impose even more significant pressure on Iran if that is what is necessary.

Senator SHAHEEN. Under Secretary Sherman, are we seeing—you referred to the Russia-Ukraine situation and responded to that. But are we seeing any fallout from what is happening in Israel and

Gaza, or also what is happening in Iraq having any impact on our negotiations?

Ms. SHERMAN. We have not to date. I cannot say that it will not in the future, but so far all of our negotiating partners have been very focused on what is happening in the negotiation room. It is not to say that on the margins there is not discussions of Ukraine, Iraq, or when we go back together what is happening horrifically in Gaza, what is happening horrifically, most importantly, to Israel's security. But so far everyone has stayed very focused on what is happening in the negotiating room.

Senator SHAHEEN. You talked about monitoring and continued inspections. What other metrics are we looking at in determining whether this is going to be a good deal for us or not?

Ms. SHERMAN. As I mentioned, Senator, the metric is really whether we have cut off every possible pathway to a nuclear weapon and whether there is assurance that their program is exclusively peaceful. So have we cut off a plutonium pathway? There are two pathways to fissile material for a nuclear weapon. One is plutonium, one is highly enriched uranium. So Natanz and Fordow are in the uranium boat and Arak in the plutonium.

Then thirdly, whether in fact we have cut off the pathways to a covert program. There is no way in any country to 100 percent guarantee that there will be no covert effort. But what you can do is have enough intrusive mechanisms to assure yourself that if there is a covert program you are going to know about it in time to stop it or that it will never get under way.

Senator SHAHEEN. Thank you.

The CHAIRMAN. Senator Risch.

Senator RISCH. Thank you, Mr. Chairman.

Ms. Sherman, in the kindest and gentlest terms previously I have urged that you do something about getting Pastor Abedini and the other two Americans released. As you know, I was incredibly critical of you guys because you cut billions loose without demanding this tiny, tiny little thing as far as Iran is concerned.

I am going to ratchet that up a little bit. You did it again. You have cut billions loose without getting those three guys released. Do me a favor, do America a favor, do the Abedini family a favor. Tell them next time you are not going to give them any more money unless they cut these three people loose.

I can almost guarantee they are going to do that. You are talking about billions of dollars and you are talking about three people that we really, really need out of prisons in Iran. Try it, just try it, and see what happens. I am willing to bet you they are going to cut those three loose in return for the money that you have available to give them.

I want to move from that, Mr. Cohen, to talk about sanctions. You know, there are a lot of us that were pretty critical about— well, very critical—about the temporary and partial relief from sanctions. We have lots and lots of concerns about it, and those concerns have not gone away.

You made a statement that I find very interesting. You said that: Well, if this thing fails, no problem; our sanctions alone will be able to do what we need to do to impose the difficulties on the Iranian economy. With all due respect, I think that that is incredibly naive.

If they sidle up to the Russians, the Chinese, the Indians, and the Turks, they can do just fine regardless of the fact that there is United States sanctions on.

I do not know how you are going to get this genie back in the bottle now that you have had this relief. I cannot imagine what that phone call is going to be like between President Obama and Mr. Putin regarding putting those sanctions back on. So I wish you well in that regard, but I think this is going to be very, very difficult if it fails. And I hope it does not fail. I hope you guys are incredibly successful. I hope that in November the Iranians say: We have changed our ways; we are going to be good people; we are not going to pursue these things. I hope you get there.

But I have, given the history we have got with this country, I have real reservations. So I wish you well in that regard, but I think you need to be thinking a little bit more deeply about how you are going to put that genie back in the bottle.

Thank you, Mr. Chairman.

The CHAIRMAN. Thank you.

Senator Coons.

Senator COONS. Thank you, Chairman Menendez, and thank you to our witnesses.

I support the administration's ongoing efforts to ensure that we completely eliminate any pathway for Iran to acquire a nuclear weapon and that we succeed in dramatically limiting their nuclear program. But I remain deeply concerned about some critical and unresolved issues in these negotiations—the status of the Arak heavy water reactor, the future of the Fordow enrichment facility, Iran's ongoing ability or hopefully lack thereof to enrich uranium, and the military dimensions of their program, including in particular those carried out at the Parchin facility.

That is why I joined Chairman Menendez and others in calling for a robust and aggressive and thorough inspections and verification regime that would include full Iranian compliance and access for inspectors, that has been unprecedented. We also called for full Iranian disclosure on the military dimensions of the nuclear program and enforcement mechanisms for a future deal, because I am convinced that if there is success in negotiations, whether in November or after the reimposition of sanctions in some next stage, we will then be in a very difficult period, where over many, many years we have to sustain sanctions, sustain an intrusive inspection regime, and keep our allies engaged with us. And over 5 or 10 or 20 years the temptation for the Iranians to cheat, given their past history, given their regional destabilizing efforts, I think will be very strong.

So if I might, first about Fordow as a facility. Secretary Kerry recently spoke of finding a different purpose for the Fordow enrichment facility that would ensure it cannot be used for nuclear weapon purposes. Could you explain what purpose Iran could possibly have for a facility constructed and configured and in the location of Fordow?

Ms. SHERMAN. I will say as much as I can in this session, Senator. There is agreement that Fordow will not be an enrichment facility, that the only enrichment facility will be Natanz, if there is an enrichment program at all. And what happens to Fordow is under discussion. There are several ideas that have been put on the table. Some of them we could probably agree to. Some of them we absolutely could not agree to. So that is a subject of negotiation.

I am happy in a classified session to tell you quite specifically what those different options are.

Senator COONS. The JPOA requires Iran agree to inspections under the IAEA additional protocol. What progress has been made and what assurances can you give us that the IAEA has the funding and the staffing, the scope and the capability, they really would need to be able to carry out over the long haul really intrusive, really reliable inspections? And have they had full access during the JPOA period and have they been denied access to any of the facilities I have referenced?

Ms. SHERMAN. The IAEA just issued a report recently in which they said that Iran had complied with all of their obligations under the JPOA, that the IAEA had had all of the access that it had asked for under the JPOA and could verify that the obligations had been met.

Indeed, when the JPOA was being finalized we obviously were in close consultation with the IAEA. They put together what they thought they would need in terms of budget to meet those additional obligations. The international community came forth quite quickly and supplied all of the money that was needed. If, in fact, we are able to get a comprehensive agreement—and, as I have said, I am not sure whether we will or not yet—I am sure the IAEA will need additional resources and I would expect the international community to come forward, because, quite frankly, any additional budget the IAEA needs is small potatoes compared to the cost of Iran having a nuclear weapon.

Senator COONS. Madam Under Secretary, I suspect you could sign—speaking for myself, you could sign me up as an enthusiastic funder of the most aggressive and searching inspection regime possible for the IAEA. Distrust and verify. Given Iran's past and current and likely future activities supporting terrorism in the region, supporting the worst sorts of regimes, and cheating on their nuclear commitments in the past, I think we should be investing heavily in a proactive inspection regime.

Ms. SHERMAN. Agreed.

Senator COONS. So, Under Secretary Cohen, that turns me to a subject we have engaged in over some time. When you testified before the Financial Services Appropriations Subcommittee in April, I asked you about the burdens facing your group, the Office of Terrorism and Financial Intelligence within Treasury. You have had the number of sanctions programs steadily expanded from, I think, 17 to 40 today, and there have been even more recent developments in terms of the scope and complexity of the sanctions we and our allies are taking on against Russia and against many other nations.

Of course, the largest and most complex of these is against Iran, and I just want to commend you again. The work that you and folks within OFAC have done——

Mr. COHEN. Thank you.

Senator COONS [continuing]. I think has made this possible.

I asked whether you needed any more resources. You demurred and said that the President's budget request was fully sufficient, as I understand in your role you should. A number of us advocated for adding additional resources. The Senate bill adds $4.5 million to your underlying budget of $102 million and the House added even more beyond that.

Do you currently really have the resources and the staff you need? I am gravely concerned that we will have great difficulty keeping together the sanctions regime over the long haul, particularly if there is some temporary relief that after an interim agreement or a long-term agreement expands. You have done a great job so far at keeping a group of unlikely allies at the table and at enforcing these sanctions. Do you not need more resources to do this?

Mr. COHEN. Well, Senator, first let me again express my appreciation, the appreciation of folks back at Treasury, for your comments and for your support. Outside of this hearing room, it is noted how much you appreciate and support our work. So I do want to convey that.

In terms of the resources, we do have sufficient resources and that is in part because we are not in this alone. We work, obviously, very closely with the State Department, very closely with elements of the intelligence community. Really, the effort with respect to Iran, with respect to Russia, the sanctions programs writ large, it is an interagency effort. We have the lead in the design and implementation and enforcement of these sanctions programs, but we draw on the resources of many others around the administration to do this.

We are stretched. I think I, the last time we spoke about this, acknowledged that people are working flat out, and they are. That is true at Treasury, it is true elsewhere as well. But we do think that we have the resources we need to ensure that our sanctions programs are effectively implemented, and we will continue to do that.

Senator COONS. Well, just in closing, I for one would like to see that we have invested everything we can, that you are not in front of us a year from now explaining that somehow the sanctions regime came unglued because we did not invest enough in it, that somehow the IAEA inspections failed to catch cheating by Iran because we did not invest enough in it.

I think there is a real chance that we will be reimposing tougher sanctions on Iran and I want to make sure that we have the abilities, skills, and resources to do it.

Thank you for your testimony today.

The CHAIRMAN. Senator Rubio.

Senator RUBIO. Thank you, Mr. Chairman. I want to thank you for holding this hearing and both of you for being here and the work you do. I want to preface what I am about to say with that. I know you have difficult work to do.

But my opinion is this entire thing is a disaster. It is not just an embarrassing diplomatic failure; this is a dangerous national security failure, in my opinion. I want to examine for a moment going into this negotiation what the goals were of both sides. I think ours are pretty transparent and clearly stated. We wanted to prevent a nuclear-armed Iran. That was our hope. That is why we had sanctions and that is why we went into this, in the hopes that Iran would say: Well, we are going to walk away from the things you need for a weapons program; we are going to prove to the world that we have changed our behavior and we are going to try to become a responsible member of the international community. That was our goal.

Their goal was different. And I believed this all along. I have said this in the past. I believe you believe this. And that is that they went into this goal, they went into this negotiation, with a simple goal: They wanted to achieve the maximum amount of sanctions relief that they could get without having to agree to any irreversible concessions on their nuclear program.

I want to examine for a moment what we have given up just to get a Joint Plan of Action. The first thing is we have implicitly agreed that they now have a right to enrich at any level. I know that we are going to argue that we can always pull that back, but we have walked away from multiple United Nations Security Council resolutions and have implicitly agreed that Iran now has a right to enrich. That is going to be the baseline for this or any future negotiation moving forward, that they now have some sort of inherent right to enrich and reprocess.

The second thing that has happened just to get a Joint Plan of Action is Iran has enjoyed real relief here. It is not just the direct sanctions that have been lifted. It is the indirect relief that they have gotten, the increases in consumer confidence and the confidence of businesses in their economy.

The third thing is it stopped the momentum. There was real international momentum on sanctions, which is what ultimately probably even brought them to the table in some respects. That momentum has now been stopped in its tracks. In fact, it is worse than that. It has now made it more difficult to reimpose sanctions in the future, to try to go back and say: If you violate this we are going to reimpose sanctions. The task of doing that has now become more difficult.

The fifth is we have left completely untouched the missiles program that they have, which they continue to develop. Let me explain to people, to the extent anyone is watching this at home, what that missile program is about. They are developing a long-range rocket that will be able to reach the United States and other places in Europe. That is what they are developing and that is what they are headed toward. There is only one reason why you develop a rocket like that and that is to put a nuclear warhead on it.

That is not mentioning they are a state sponsor of terrorism. There is no nation on Earth that uses terrorism more than they do as an element of statecraft.

So let us back up and look at Iran's point of view in this whole thing. They now have achieved an acknowledged right that did not used to exist, an acknowledged right to enrich. They have stopped the momentum on more sanctions. They have made future sanctions even harder. They are not concerned about the United States carrying out any military action against them. In fact, I would say they view it as almost a near impossibility at this stage.

I know we are going to hear all this talk about, well, you know, this whole thing is contingent on other things and bragging about all the things that can be in a future deal. A nuclear weapon program has three critical components: enrichment, weaponization, and the delivery of that weapon. On enrichment, we have now given them an acknowledged right to keep that capacity. On weaponization, that has been outsourced to the IAEA, which has already said they are having trouble getting into some of these sites, like some of the secret military sites of the past. They will not even show us what they did in the past. And I have already talked about how the missiles remain untouched.

And by the way, if they violate—let us say you do reach a deal with them. If they violate any component of this, it will all be based on our ability to do two things: find that violation and punish that violation. In the finding of that violation, we are dealing with a government that has consistently had a secret program.

And I promise you they will rope-a-dope us. You can think you are going to have inspectors crawling all over the place. They can rope-a-dope us for months at a time. Hopefully the world is—in their mind, hopefully the world is distracted by some other crisis somewhere on the planet and they rope-a-dope us on the inspection element of it.

On reimposing sanctions, well, reimposing international sanctions, let me tell you how hard that is going to be. The Russians, or at least the separatists that they are arming, just shot down a commercial airplane. They just killed almost 300 innocent civilians. And we have had to drag our allies and others kicking and screaming just to increase sanctions a little bit more. So how hard do you think it is going to be to reimpose sanctions on this thing if it falls apart?

I just think the danger here is quite frank. We are going to wake up one day—after this administration is long gone, some future President or future administration is going to wake up one day and realize they have had a secret weaponization program all along, all they have to do is flip the switch now on the enrichment capability, they have a long-range weapon that they can arm, they are either a threshold nuclear power or in fact become a nuclear power.

At that point what will we have? A country that now has spread their influence of terrorism so they can asymmetrically attack those who seek to impose sanctions against them, a sanctions regime that fell apart years ago and is almost impossible to put back together, with Europeans and other countries now heavily invested in their economy, a country that will basically have a nuclear weapon—think of North Korea, but motivated by radical Islamic beliefs—with the capability to hit major United States cities, not to mention our allies in Europe, and of course Israel.

And by the way, all these rockets that are landing in Israel from Gaza, guess where they came from, many of them? From Iran. That is what these people do.

So look, I think we all hope and wish that this thing would work out, but I think there are very few among us on this committee that think that it will. And I am sad that we are going to be wrong about it. And I am also sad that anyone who criticizes this deal is often characterized as a warmonger, that we just want to go to war and carpet bomb people.

On the contrary, here is what I do not want to see: I do not want to see us fall into a situation where sanctions is no longer an option because you cannot put it back together and now war is the only option, because war is a terrible thing, it is a horrible thing. The only thing worse than war is crazy people with a nuclear weapon that can reach the United States of America on a rocket. That is the only thing that is worse than a war with regard to this situation.

I hope I am wrong. I do not believe that I am. And I fear, Mr. Chairman, that some day soon we will wake up to the reality that they have done a North Korea on us, they have acquired a nuclear weapon, they can hold the world hostage with that weapon, and there is very few or little we can do about it.

Senator MCCAIN. Mr. Chairman, Mr. Chairman.

The CHAIRMAN. Yes, Senator?

Senator MCCAIN. Would my dear friend from California allow me 30 seconds to make a statement? I have to go.

Senator BOXER. Absolutely.

Senator MCCAIN. I appreciate that.

The CHAIRMAN. Senator McCain.

Senator MCCAIN. Mr. Chairman, it has become obvious to me and even more obvious in the hearing here today that this is really in every aspect a treaty that is being considered with Iran, and I believe it requires the advice and consent of the United States Senate and I hope we can move forward with legislation that would require that.

I thank you, Mr. Chairman. I thank my friend from California.

The CHAIRMAN. Senator Boxer.

Senator BOXER. Mr. Chairman, thank you and Senator Corker for holding this hearing.

I do not have questions for the panel because my staff has told me while I was at another hearing my questions were responded to. So I will go over those.

But I have to say that some of the language I just heard from Senator Rubio—I wish he was here—brings back the rhetoric of days past. We do not want the smoking gun to be a mushroom cloud. I think the whole issue that we face is so complicated that we have to, I believe, strongly support these diplomatic efforts so that none of that does come true.

The whole world is watching. So this is an opportunity to prevent Iran from acquiring a nuclear weapon. I have said many times that we have an obligation, our generation—we are here now—to test this window of opportunity. That is all it is.

And I think the administration has been really honest about it. As I remember, the President himself said there is a 50–50 chance. You know, a 50–50 chance. So it may not work out and all the hyper rhetoric may be something we turn to and more. But right now we have an obligation to test this window, because I think it is in our national interest, the benefit of our kids, the kids of the world, and in the interests of our allies in the region like Israel.

And I think our language should reflect that, although we are very skeptical, we are very supportive of this opportunity. Israel's security is threatened on so many fronts, from terrorists in Gaza launching rockets and digging tunnels and all the things we know about. We also know the rise of ISIS in Syria is a horrible threat. So the opportunity, as the world moves in a bad direction, to focus our attention on something good, I do not think it should be lost.

I know how hard our negotiators have been working, tirelessly, on a comprehensive agreement. I know it is tough. It is incredibly difficult and complex, which is why we have another extension. I just want to be on the record, in the midst of these sensitive negotiations, I am not going to force the administration into a corner by dictating a preferred outcome or prematurely ratcheting up any sanctions, because we have got lots of time to do that. And I think trying to attach language on Iran to other bills, as I have faced with the U.S.-Israel Strategic Partnership Act—that ought to be a clean bill and not be burdened by this incredibly sensitive, complicated matter.

I want to be clear, and I have written my own letters. I have not gone on the letters that have 80 signatures. I have said any final agreement must be air-tight, it must be verifiable, and it must be long-lasting. We cannot accept anything less because we cannot trust Iran. We all know that. And if Iran walks away from the negotiating table it will be a sad day for them, too, because we will all come together in support of a robust U.S. and international response that includes the immediate restoration of any suspended sanctions and additional, biting sanctions on Iran.

I would go further and make it clear, so let everyone hear my voice, this Senator, that all options have to be on the table should Iran attempt to continue its illicit nuclear program, and I mean all options.

So the next 4 months are critical, and I hope and pray that they will result in a comprehensive final agreement that is acceptable to the United States and to our allies and that brings a peaceful end to this nuclear program.

This is a historic chance. We could let it pass us by or we can all work together, being very clear, it is worth a chance. We see how easy it is to go to war. We see that all over the globe. And may I hasten to add, some of my colleagues I have heard in at least 6 to 10 cases say: Go to war, America, go to war, America.

We need to resolve these issues, and war is a last resort, not a first resort. So this is an opportunity that we have. I do not want to gloss over how hard it is. I share the 50–50 view. Could go one way, could go the other. But lord, if we can have it going the right way I think we should be very supportive.

I just want to say this to you, Wendy. I call you "Wendy" because you are my buddy. I think it is very important to keep Congress informed, and I think some of the complaints that we hear are legitimate complaints. We know it is hard. We know there are details. We know you are working 24/7. But in the kind of government that we have, we are all in this together. It used to be foreign policy stopped at the water's edge. It is not that way, for whatever reason. It is not that way. That means it is even more important that you let us know every twist and turn, because at the end of the day I do not think that there are any of us that would turn away from a solid, verifiable agreement. And at the end of the day there are not any of us that will not use all the tools at our disposal if there is no agreement. So how important it is for you to keep us informed.

That is my statement, and I thank you.

The CHAIRMAN. Senator Flake.

Senator FLAKE. Thank you. I appreciate this hearing and I appreciate the testimony.

I am among those who believes that we ought to test every opportunity. I think this is an opportunity. It may not bear fruit, but I think it is incumbent on us to test it, and I applaud the administration for doing so.

I just want to clarify a couple of numbers that came out. Mr. Cohen, you had mentioned the amount of sanctions relief that they had taken advantage of, but I have got a $3 to $4 billion figure. Is that what is expected with the extension of the JPOA or what they have realized so far? I know the initial estimates were about $8 to $9 billion. Can you tell us how much they have taken advantage of and how much will be taken advantage of over the next couple months?

Mr. COHEN. Certainly, Senator. The $3 to $4 billion figure that I referenced in my oral testimony is our top end estimate of what Iran may enjoy in terms of sanctions relief in the next 4 months. That is comprised of the $2.8 billion in its own restricted assets that it will be getting access to over the course of the next 4 months and then some figures for additional petrochemical sales and auto exports, which we estimate will be worth about $500 million altogether.

So the low end of that estimate is about $3.3 billion. Obviously, precisely how Iran is able to take advantage of the continued suspension of the petrochemical and the auto sanctions is an estimate. We will see how it turns out.

For the initial JPOA period, initial 6 months, our estimate going in was that Iran would enjoy about $6 to $7 billion as a maximum in terms of its relief. I think that estimate was actually overstated. Our best figures are that Iran earned or enjoyed a little over 5 billion dollars' worth of relief in the JPOA period, no relief on the petrochemicals suspension, very, very little in terms of the auto sanctions.

Senator FLAKE. And the reason for that is it is difficult for them to take advantage of it because of the interlocking nature of the sanctions that are out there, is that right?

Mr. COHEN. That is right. One key fact is that Iran remains cut off from the international financial system. So even though it is now not sanctionable to engage in petrochemical sales or auto sales with Iran, it is still difficult to find financial institutions to do that work.

Senator FLAKE. I think we all acknowledge the reason that Iran is at the table is because of the effectiveness of these sanctions, and I would submit it is largely because it has been Iran versus the West rather than Iran versus just the United States. So it is important to keep our allies on board here.

Do you have a concern—I will address this to Ms. Sherman. Do you have a concern that if we were to not extend and not continue with these negotiations, that our allies may cut their own deal or move on without us?

Ms. SHERMAN. Senator, listening to some of your colleagues, I wrote down: "Without diplomacy, we will not be able to keep the sanctions together," which is exactly your point, that, in fact, we certainly should not have proceeded with an extension if we did not think there was some significant progress and the possibility of a comprehensive agreement. We should have called it a day.

But, having seen some progress and heading in the right direction and seeing the possibility that we might get to a comprehensive agreement, though I do not know the end of the story yet, we thought it was critical to take diplomacy to the very last possible promise that we might get to a comprehensive agreement, because that does keep the international community united in the enforcement of sanctions.

If our partners and even those who are not so much our partners saw that we were going to cut diplomacy short, then those sanctions enforcement would have frayed much more quickly.

So we do not have any guarantees here. I do not know that we will get to an agreement at the end of these 4 months. But I do agree with your point that without going this extra mile, given that there was some significant progress in the talks, we would have a much harder time keeping the sanctions together. And I think Under Secretary Cohen, since he is nodding, does agree.

Senator FLAKE. Thank you for making that point. I am concerned that when these sanctions fray, if they fray, then it will not be as effective. Unilateral sanctions very seldom work and we have got to keep the community together. That is why I think it is important to explore the diplomacy avenue as much as we can.

Is there a concern among the Iranians that we get to the end of this and the ability of the United States to deliver on sanctions relief is in question, given what Members of Congress have said? And will the administration come back to Congress for statutory relief of these sanctions, or what is going to be the mechanism in your view at that point if an agreement is reached?

Ms. SHERMAN. Let me start and let Under Secretary Cohen then comment. I can assure every Member of the United States Senate and of the House of Representatives that Congress is a constant topic of conversation by the Iranians. They are well aware of Congress' authorities, not only in terms of oversight, but in terms of legislation.

We have been very clear that initially there will only be suspension of any of our sanctions regime and of the international community's, that the lifting of sanctions, for which we must return to Congress for statutory relief, will only come when certain benchmarks verified by the IAEA are reached, and they are very serious and substantive benchmarks, because this has to be a durable agreement and it will only be durable if the United States Congress and other institutions and governments around the world believe that the compliance is real and sustainable over a period of time.

Senator FLAKE. I hope the Iranians do understand that if an agreement is reached that is verifiable that we will follow through with sanctions relief. I hope they also understand that if we do not reach an agreement, that existing sanctions will be enforced and additional sanctions will be added. But I think both sides of that equation need to be understood.

Did you have something to add?

Mr. COHEN. Only, Senator, that in the course of this Joint Plan of Action we have committed to certain suspensions of sanctions, and one of the things that we have done to sort of reinforce the point both that we will continue to enforce the sanctions that are in place as well as in good faith fulfill our commitments on the release side, is to take very seriously what we have committed to on the sanctions relief, so that the Iranians as they go into these negotiations can understand that there is potential light at the end of this tunnel if they take the steps necessary.

So we have been I think working very hard on both sides of the coin, as you describe.

Senator FLAKE. Thank you.

The CHAIRMAN. Senator Markey.

Senator MARKEY. Thank you, Mr. Chairman.

Ambassador Sherman, there has been a lot of discussion amongst nuclear nonproliferation experts about the potential for a proliferation cascade in the Middle East if Iran were to obtain a nuclear weapon. It is critical that the current negotiations succeed in preventing Iran from developing a weapon, but even if under a final agreement Iran retains a domestic uranium enrichment capability I am concerned that this could still raise fears in the region and prompt other states to reconsider their contingency plans and nuclear posture.

It has been reported that both Saudi Arabia and Jordan are interested in pursuing nuclear cooperation agreements with the United States. How will we be able to convince these countries, our partners, to agree not to demand the right to enrich uranium as part of these agreements if we allow Iran to maintain its enrichment capability, especially since we just concluded a nuclear cooperation agreement with Vietnam that allows Vietnam to enrich uranium as well?

Ms. SHERMAN. Thank you, Senator. There is no question that our consultations with partners and allies in the region is quite critical to ensure that we do not have a proliferation cascade in any way, shape, or form. Part of that will be if indeed there is a comprehensive agreement with Iran and they do have a very small, limited domestic program, that it be very small, that it be very limited, that it be subject to intrusive monitoring mechanisms, so that there are not incentives for other countries to want to proceed down that road.

As you know, the United States does not recognize that any country has a right to enrichment. We do not believe that is a right under the NPT and we will continue to vigorously enforce that perspective.

Senator MARKEY. Again, I want to comment on the Iran Government leadership recently claims that the country will need an industrial-scale enrichment capability to generate nuclear power. The interim deal stated that in a final agreement Iran's enrichment program would be, ''consistent with practical needs.'' This is a country with the second-largest natural gas reserves in the world. As I have noted before several times in this committee, Iran flares off, wastes that is, the equivalent of 13 nuclear reactors' worth of natural gas each year, which they could use to produce electricity.

So I urge you to keep in mind as we negotiate over what Iran's practical needs for nuclear power are that it is a very duplicitous game that they are playing, since they flare the natural gas that our country uses for electrical generation and many other countries in the world. So we should just be deeply skeptical that there is any legitimate civilian purpose in this enrichment program, and I just want to again continue to make that point.

The nuclear cooperation agreement that we have with the United Arab Emirates includes a commitment by the United Arab Emirates not to enrich uranium or reprocess spent fuel, but it also allows for the agreement to be renegotiated if other countries in the region get more favorable terms. So if Jordan or Saudi Arabia demand the right to enrich or reprocess in response to an inadequate Iran agreement, the UAE could make the demand as well since that is part of the agreement.

Is it not possible that a final agreement with Iran that allows enrichment to continue will cause a proliferation cascade in the region as other countries begin their own programs?

Ms. SHERMAN. As I said, Senator, we are very well aware of the potential risks of any agreement that allows any country to enrich, because we do not believe that any country has a right. We also believe that fuel is available on the open market for power generation. So if indeed we reach a comprehensive agreement, and that is not a sure thing at all, and there is an enrichment program in Iran, we believe it must be very small, very limited, attached to a practical need. That certainly would not be industrial-size capacity, to be sure. Indeed, Iran has talked about Bushehr, which is fueled by Russia. We believe Russia should continue that commitment and it has committed to do so and Iran does not need to have an enrichment program to provide fuel for Bushehr.

So we agree with your concern and so therefore we believe that this should be a very limited, very small, attached to a practical need, under very intrusive monitoring that would be a disincentive for any other country to want a similar program.

Senator MARKEY. I appreciate that. And again, this Vietnam agreement does allow Vietnam to enrich and I just think it does create a precedent that is a very small step from something that is much more profound.

Are you concerned that other regional players, such as Turkey or Egypt, would seek to develop their own uranium enrichment capabilities, and how could that impact regional tensions?

Ms. SHERMAN. We certainly hope that no one goes down this road. We are trying to create incentives to do otherwise and disincentives to proceed in this manner. We think that there are much more economical ways to get fuel for power generation and would not encourage any country to go down this road. Clearly, we want to make sure that we have in place tremendous compliance risks for Iran should we get to a comprehensive agreement if they do not comply.

Senator MARKEY. Again, the greater the enrichment program in Iran is, the greater the risk then that there is a transfer of that material into other countries or subnational groups that could be used against American interests. So the smaller the program, obviously the more likely that we will not see that kind of a diversion.

So again, we are very close now to reaching that cascading point, and we have held it off for decades, since President Kennedy warned us about it. We have pretty much held the number of countries to a very small number.

In a June report, the U.N. panel of experts that monitors Iran's sanctions reminded us that Iran continues to maintain wide-reaching transnational illicit procurement networks. It uses front companies to obtain materials on the global market for its nuclear and missile programs under the guise of legitimate commerce. These are complex operations, including transport, shipping agents, freight forwarders, warehouses, and airlines, and they violate U.N. Security Council Resolution 1737, passed in 2006, which bans the provision of items to Iran that could be used in its nuclear and missile programs.

If Iran gains further sanctions relief and expands international trade as part of a nuclear deal, what challenges would that pose to our efforts to disrupt this facilitation and procurement network which exists even today?

Mr. COHEN. Senator, that U.N. report is exactly right. Iran does continue to try to illicitly acquire material through these procurement networks. We continue to identify and disrupt those networks where we find them and have taken action in the last several months to disrupt some of these networks.

Going forward, if there is an agreement one of the issues that we will confront and that we are focused on is how to ensure during the course of this long-term agreement, if there is one to be had, that we are able to continue to ensure that the Security Council resolutions and our own sanctions on proliferation activity are respected as the agreement rolls out.

Senator MARKEY. Let me just ask very quickly: At the Parchin military base, given Iran's ongoing efforts to hide incriminating evidence by paving over the site with asphalt, do you agree that gaining access to this facility is an increasingly urgent priority? They are acting, Iran, in a very suspicious fashion.

Ms. SHERMAN. We are concerned about all of the things Iran does to avoid their obligations under the NPT and their obligations to U.N. Security Council resolutions and the IAEA systems analysis that is under way, and Parchin is certainly a critical element of that.

Senator MARKEY. Will a final agreement include Parchin, so that we can be sure that there is no clandestine activity occurring at that site?

Ms. SHERMAN. The final agreement will include the IAEA being satisfied that the possible military dimensions of Iran's program have been addressed.

Senator MARKEY. So that includes the inspections?

Ms. SHERMAN. From the IAEA's perspective, that is certainly where they are today.

Senator MARKEY. Thank you.

Thank you, Mr. Chairman.

The CHAIRMAN. Senator Corker for a final comment.

Senator CORKER. Thank you, Mr. Chairman, and thanks for having this hearing and for all your work on Iran and its nuclear activities.

I want to thank the witnesses again for being here. For those in the listening audience, one of the natural questions one would ask is, what are the gaps now between where we want to be and where we want to close. We have obviously had those kinds of Q&A in another setting and obviously we realize that in an open setting that is not a good thing to have discussed. But I do want to say, look, I know Senator Flake mentioned that he believes this is a historic opportunity. Look, I do too. I think all of us—I think you know that everyone up here really does want to see a diplomatic solution, and everyone appreciates the work that all of you are doing.

I think that when the JPOA came out and basically acknowledged enrichment you saw some—it elicited pretty strong responses from all involved. As Senator Markey was just mentioning, we just went through some 123 agreements with other countries. Here we are pushing our friends to not enrich, and yet we open these negotiations acknowledging enrichment. So there are a lot of concerns. All of us wish you success. There are a lot of concerns.

I do want to just close by saying this, though. In spite of the fact that we want you to be successful—I heard what you said today and in essence you said there is no deadline. I know, I know you have got to fudge a little bit because you do not know what is going to happen. But I think in essence it was said there is not a deadline, and I hope there is a deadline.

Ms. SHERMAN. Our intent is to end this the 24th of November.

Senator CORKER. I know you talked about double-digit minimum length. I just want to say—and I know that maybe that is better said in a classified setting. But I just want to say again, unless it is really, really long we have done nothing, we have done nothing.

The goalposts are moving a little bit, I mean, even relative to what you guys are saying you are going to do with Congress, the acknowledgment that in essence you are going to have a conversation. Rose Gottemoeller called me this morning at 8:30 and we had a conversation about the violations of the INF Treaty that we have known about for some time because we access classified documents. But I read about it last night in the New York Times.

That is not exactly the kind of consultation we expect. It is not lost on us that at the end of this, even though it coincides with when the JPOA began or discussions began. They end on November the 24th, which is likely beyond the ending of any lame duck session that may occur after the election. That does not go lost on us.

So I would just say that, again, it appears to me that what you are saying is that you are going to do whatever you wish to do, you are not going to consult Congress, you do not believe that that is your responsibility. You are going to have a conversation with us, but we are not going to really have the ability, even though we put these sanctions in place—and by the way, it was my amendment in Banking that pushed this to multilateral types of sanctions which you have pursued.

But again, I think what you have said today is that Congress is relevant relative to raising concerns, not relevant relative to whether this is going to be approved by Congress or sanctions waived. I just think that that is something that all of us who serve in this body—this is one of the biggest agreements that will likely be entered into, if we enter into one, and in essence Congress is playing no role other than raising questions.

So, Mr. Chairman, I hope that there is some way that we will figure out to deal with that. I think that is a major lapse in our responsibilities. And I thank you for your continued concern about this issue, and thank the witnesses for their work. But the goalposts are moving.

Ms. SHERMAN. With all due respect, Senator, I take the prerogatives of the United States Congress incredibly seriously, as does President Obama and Secretary Kerry, and we do not believe it is merely a conversation. We believe it is a consultation. We believe you have oversight authorities. We believe you have legislative authorities.

We have worked very closely to provide you with real-time information, often in classified sessions because there is an ongoing negotiation, which we are very appreciative that you have permitted. We will continue to do so. It is in our interest that Congress know what we are doing every step of this negotiation and it is very critical that the United States of America be one, Congress and the administration working together, if we are to achieve a comprehensive agreement and then to carry out that comprehensive agreement durably over a sustained period of time that gives us all the assurance that every pathway to a nuclear weapon is closed off and that their program is entirely peaceful. I quite agreed with your opening statement and the chairman's that we all share the same goal.

The CHAIRMAN. I had said final words, but Senator Paul has returned and I want to accommodate him. So Senator Paul.

Senator PAUL. Thank you very much.

Secretary Sherman, how significant is it that the Iranians have now converted their 20 percent stockpile to 5 percent?

Ms. SHERMAN. What they have done is taken their up-to-20 percent and either diluted it or oxidized it, and under the extension they are going to take 25 kilograms—that is about 20, 25 percent of what they have of the oxidized up-to-20 percent—and turn it into metal plates for the Teheran research reactor, which means the likelihood of it being reconverted back to enriched uranium is extremely low.

All of that is very important. They will in addition, as a result of this extension, oxidize all their up-to-2 percent stockpile, which is over 3 metric tons. Although it does not have significant what we call SWU's, separative work units, which is the way that you talk about the energy in this material, in a breakout scenario it would be significant. So we are glad both those things are being done.

All of that said, we are of course concerned about their up-to-5 percent stockpile. That is capped under the JPOA, but we will want to deal with that stockpile and every other kind of stockpile they have as a part of any comprehensive agreement.

Senator PAUL. But you would call it a significant evidence of compliance, converting the 20 to 5?

Ms. SHERMAN. Well, actually they have oxidized or diluted their entire up-to-20 percent stockpile and the IAEA has said that they have met their obligation.

Senator PAUL. What is the administration's position on the Menendez-Corker bill to institute more sanctions? I believe also part of the bill is that there would be no right of any enrichment; whether or not this would be persuasive and to be a cudgel that entices or encourages them to do what they need to do or whether or not it would push them away from the negotiating table?

Ms. SHERMAN. We believe, Senator, that we believe at this point it would push them away from the negotiating table and, quite importantly, it would probably push our P5+1 colleagues away from the negotiating table. So although I have great respect for the chairman and for Senator Corker and for all the Members of the U.S. Senate and I believe the intentions here are all absolutely right on, which is to keep the pressure on Iran to do what is necessary here to give the international community the assurance we are looking for and to cut off all the pathways to nuclear weapons, the administration believes quite strongly that at this moment in this negotiation additional legislative action would potentially derail the negotiation, and that Iran is quite clear that the Congress will pass legislation at any moment that it is deemed absolutely necessary to do so.

Senator PAUL. Can you quantify how much this going from 20 to 5 delays the breakout time? Is that quantifiable? Does it make it 6 months, the breakout time? Does it add 5 months? Is it quantifiable?

Ms. SHERMAN. What I prefer, Senator, if I could, is in terms of specific breakout times and elements, to have the intelligence community brief that in a classified setting.

Senator PAUL. But it is—you say it delays it? It obviously has to be a step in the right direction to go from 20 to 5.

Ms. SHERMAN. Every element that we can deal with helps on breakout, but until we get a comprehensive agreement we will not have a durable agreement that will give us the kind of assurance we are looking for.

Senator PAUL. And it is another significant step going from oxides to fuel plates?

Ms. SHERMAN. It is an important step, because the ability to turn it back into enriched material is that much more difficult, yes.

Senator PAUL. Thank you.

Thank you, Mr. Chairman.

The CHAIRMAN. Well, thank you both. Let me just conclude with some summary thoughts. We all appreciate your service. No one here questions that. It is only because of the importance of the issue that everybody feels as they do.

Let me just make a comment. There is a difference—and I think we have gotten better at this. But you know, notification is different than consultation. Notification is when you tell us, we are doing X, Y, or Z. Consultation is when you say, we are doing X, Y, or Z and what do you think, and how do you incorporate some legitimate views so that if and when you get to a final agreement people will have a sense of confidence on that.

So I just urge you to think about not just telling us what you are doing, but consulting in a way in which there is input taking place that when it can be agreed upon can be incorporated.

Secondly, on the sanctions, I heard your response and I will just say once again for the record, the problem—of course the Iranians know we will pass sanctions if they do not agree. It is the lead time that will be necessary. Every sanctions that I have authored with other colleagues has required a minimum of 6 months notification to the international community and to businesses, and then the process of setting them into enforcement and enforcing them takes longer.

Unfortunately, that amount of time is greater than the amount of time for breakout if the Iranians determine that they want to break out. So that is the fundamental conflict I have about saying we can wait, but the consequences of the impact of those sanctions will be less so.

There would be no greater Thanksgiving Day gift than for you to all be successful, for our country, I believe for the Iranian people, and for the world. But the concerns here I think are very legitimate. In our next panel that is going to come up, which is an excellent panel, I look at the testimony of Mr. Heinonen, who spent 27 years as the Deputy Director of the IAEA, well respected. One of the things he says in his testimony: As the Iranian Ambassador's recent letter to the IAEA demonstrates, Iran continues to challenge, inter alia, the agency's right and obligation to verify the correctness and completeness of Iran's declarations under the comprehensive safeguards agreement, the legality of the IAEA board's resolutions, and the IAEA Secretariat's practices in reporting its findings in its reports to the IAEA board and the U.N. Security Council."

Now, that letter was just June the 4th of 2014. So you say to yourself, wow, they are challenging basically everything the IAEA is doing and yet we are in the midst of negotiations thinking that on some of the key questions we have discussed, like the military dimensions of their program, we are going to get there in 4 months when you do not start actually negotiating—maybe there is something going on in between, but you are not meeting until September.

Secondly, I appreciate what Treasury has been doing, but even despite what you are doing, part of the challenge that we face is that, yes, Iran's economy is bad, but it is better than it was. And that is part of the positive, that sentiment that is created by virtue of the Joint Plan of Action and its extension which is helping in my perspective to create some modest growth.

You know, GDP is expected to grow at 2 percent. That is modest, but it is a huge improvement over Iran's economic performance in the 2012–13 fiscal year, when GDP contracted by 6.6 percent. Inflation is beginning to go down the first quarter of 2013, so the rate of inflation dipped below 20 percent, a worrisome number, but certainly less than half of the inflation that it was at 45 percent. The rial has gone up in its value. The stock market has gone up in its value.

So there are consequences for—positive consequences for Iran, negative for what we consider the continuing of pressure to get them to do the right thing.

Finally, you know, I spent a fair amount of time reading—and I will not talk about which of my friends in the press with their editorials. But I went back and read years of editorials about North Korea. And my God, it was amazing to me that the language that was used about the aspirations that we were seeking in North Korea is the language—I do not know whether it is the same editors, but it is the language that is being used now as it relates to Iran.

And to be very honest with you, if there is an example of that ''no deal is better than a bad deal,'' from my perspective it is the framework agreement that was devised with North Korea, because it failed to dismantle its illicit nuclear infrastructure, it limited inspections to a singular nuclear complex. And we all thought it was a success. Then we later learned that North Korea repeatedly cheated on the deal. Then they quit the deal, then they detonated their first nuclear explosion. We cannot have that as it relates to Iran.

So look, I am glad to hear that you say the Iranians pay attention to Congress. If they want to pay attention to Congress, they should let go of Dr. Abedini and every other American they have hostage. That would send a hell of a message.

Secondly, only because the stakes are so high that the passions are so strong—so we have a deep respect for what you both and those who work with you are doing and we have a mutual goal. I believe we have a role to play to help you with that mutual goal. You may not always like it, but I think at the end of the day it is positive.

With the thanks of the committee, this panel is excused. Let me call our next panel: Dr. Olli Heinonen, who is a senior fellow for research at the Belfer Center for Science and International Affairs at the Harvard Kennedy School of Government; and Mr. Michael Singh, who is the Lane-Swig Senior Fellow and managing director of the Washington Institute.

We want to thank our witnesses who are leaving and those who are joining with them. We would ask you to do so quietly. We want to tell our new panel that your full statements will be included in the record without objection and we would like you to summarize more or less in 5 minutes so that we can have the type of give and take we just had with our first panel.

I would like to also announce that Dr. Gary Samore, who was listed on the hearing notice to be a witness, unfortunately took ill today and so we do not have the benefit of his expertise today, but we hope to do so at some other time.

Dr. Heinonen.

STATEMENT OF OLLI HEINONEN, PH.D., SENIOR FELLOW FOR RESEARCH AT THE BELFER CENTER FOR SCIENCE AND INTERNATIONAL AFFAIRS, HARVARD KENNEDY SCHOOL OF GOVERNMENT, CAMBRIDGE, MA

Dr. HEINONEN. Thank you. Chairman Menendez, Ranking Member Corker, members of the committee, thank you for inviting me to address this hearing.

Since 2002 we have experienced many adverse actions taken by Iran. Iran has not suspended its enrichment and heavy water reactor-related activities, not cooperated with the IAEA on outstanding issues, particularly with those which raise concerns on the military dimensions of Iran's nuclear program. The implementation of the JPOA has generally proceeded well, but the negotiations have also seen headwinds.

The Iranian Ambassador's letter in June to the IAEA demonstrates that Iran continues to challenge the agency's right and obligation to verify the correctness and completeness of declarations, the legality of the IAEA board resolutions, and the IAEA's Secretariat's practices in reporting its findings.

Due to the fact that Iran has been running parts of its nuclear program first clandestinely and without fulfilling its NPT reporting obligations and disregarding Security Council resolutions, the onus of proof bears heavily on Iran to show that its nuclear program is entirely peaceful.

I have recently published with David Albright and Andrea Sticker an analysis on five principles which the negotiators crafting the comprehensive agreement should follow. I highlight some of those basic principles.

The first one: Stable provisions. It is important for the credibility and durability of an agreement to minimize the opportunities for violations and delays to achieve compliance. The first requirement is that Iran provides a complete declaration of its past and current nuclear program, which then will serve as a clearcut baseline for the verification and monitoring activities to be conducted by the IAEA.

Another important provision is the technical parameters of the nuclear program. An example of what would create an unstable and highly reversible situation is, for instance, suggestions that involve lowering the amount of enriched uranium in Iran while increasing the number of allowed centrifuges to 10,000 or more IR–1's in order to increase the breakout times.

Keeping enriched uranium stocks exceedingly low would be impossible in practice. Practicalities of operating a centrifuge plant and a uranium conversion or fuel production plants would lead to larger enriched uranium stocks, compromising the goal of longer breakout times.

Experiences from various agreements since 2003 also demonstrate the importance of unambiguous baselines for monitoring of Iran's undertakings. Ambiguity in parameters leads to potential slippage.

With regard to the practical needs, I would pass them here, but they are in the written text and go straight to the effective verification.

Timely detection and prevention of the development and acquisition of nuclear weapons or a state's capability to produce them is a complex task. There are things which we know and there are aspects of such programs which we perhaps can to a certain degree deduce, but also features which we do not know.

The IAEA must provide prompt warning of violations, determine the correctness and completeness of declarations, establish the total number of centrifuges acquired by Iran and the size of its natural and enriched uranium stocks, and establish confidence in the absence of undeclared nuclear material and activities, including assurances on the absence of nuclear weapons-related efforts.

The long-term agreement must establish a range of other verification provisions, also referred to as Additional Protocol Plus.

Moreover, military sites do not form sanctuaries. The IAEA has right to conduct inspections on those under the existing agreements when appropriate. Iran has to provide the IAEA with unconditional and unrestricted access to all areas, facilities, equipment, records, people, and materials which IAEA needs to do its work.

Adequate verification also requires Iran to verifiably stop its efforts to procure key proliferation-sensitive goods illegally for its nuclear program. If not stopped, Iran could secretly acquire such items for clandestine activities.

To ensure that the IAEA has the necessary legally binding authorities to conduct the additional verification work, the agreement between P5+1 and Iran should be endorsed by the U.N. Security Council.

Possible military dimensions. Iran's most serious verification shortcoming remains its unwillingness to address the IAEA's concerns about past and possibly ongoing military dimensions of its nuclear programs. For the IAEA to conclude that all nuclear material is in peaceful use, this is not possible unless Iran satisfies the IAEA in this key area.

Unless properly addressed, it would be difficult to create a meaningful and robust verification regime for Iran. Such additional long-term monitoring took place in South Africa from 1993 until 2010 until the then-IAEA was able to conclude that all nuclear material was in peaceful use.

Irreversibility. Irreversibility is the heart of the dispute about Iran limiting plutonium production at the Arak nuclear reactor. The simple fix is for Iran to remove the currently installed core and replace it with a smaller one not able to hold enough natural uranium to run the reactor. With these changes to the Arak reactor, there will be also no need for heavy water production. Regular, light water could be used in this reactor and heavy water could be shipped out.

Iran has also resisted making concessions about what to do with the centrifuges that would exceed a cap on the total agreed number of installed centrifuges. If not removed and rendered harmless, Iran could within months reconstitute operations and create a sizable breakout capability.

Adequate response time, the last point. An agreement must provide sufficient time to mount an effective response to major violations by Iran. IAEA reports form a key part of the monitoring of compliance. The member states can use these detailed reports to complement their findings from their activities conducted by national means.

While breakout time does not include the total time to produce a nuclear weapon, the production of weapon-grade uranium is the more difficult and time-consuming portion of making a nuclear weapon. Once Iran has enough weapon-grade uranium at its disposal, material would vanish and go to covert sites for further weaponization efforts, which could be small in size, without visible detectable signatures, as was the case in South Africa.

In summary, the actual verification process will be time-consuming and will stretch over many years, especially more so for a nuclear program that had been largely clandestine in nature and complex. It took the IAEA for medium-sized nuclear programs in European countries with a comprehensive safeguards agreement and additional protocol implemented about 5 years to conclude that all nuclear material in these countries was in peaceful use.

Forthcoming and proper cooperation from Iran could set a tone for the country to have in place a limited nuclear program. A meaningful and robust verification system with additional authorities endorsed by the U.N. Security Council is needed to support a long-term deal.

Thank you.

[The prepared statement of Dr. Heinonen follows:]

PREPARED STATEMENT OF DR. OLLI HEINONEN

Chairman Menendez, Ranking Member Corker, distinguished members of the committee, thank you for inviting me to address this hearing on "Iran: Status of the P–5+1."

In my testimony, I will focus on the verification aspects of elements needed in a comprehensive nuclear agreement with Iran, which is being negotiated as a next stage to the Joint Plan of Action (JPOA) concluded in Geneva on 24 November

I base my remarks on the implementation of the comprehensive safeguards agreement (CSA) and relevant U.N. Security Council resolutions on Iran, recent experiences from the implementation of the JPOA, and complemented with personal experience drawn additionally and in particular, from the IAEA verification activities in South Africa after its dismantlement of its nuclear weapons program, Libya, Syria, and North Korea.

When we look at the lessons learned on nuclear proliferation cases of the last couple of decades, states have chosen to use undeclared nuclear materials at undeclared locations or facilities at declared sites to which the IAEA had not had full access. Proliferators also took advantage of weaknesses at the front end of the nuclear fuel cycle by exploiting the use of yellow cake for uranium conversion at undeclared facilities. In order to achieve their objectives, states often, in addition to secrecy, stalled, misled or obfuscated to buy time and delay the IAEA in its verification mission. Since 2002, we have experienced many of these adverse actions taken by Iran. Iran has not heeded to the resolutions of the United Nations Security Council,[2] which have asked it, inter alia, to suspend all enrichment-related and heavy water-related activities, and to cooperate with the IAEA on all outstanding issues, particularly with those which raise concerns on the military dimension of Iran's nuclear program.[3] Both the implementation of the JPOA and the Framework on Cooperation[4] have generally proceeded well, but negotiations have also seen headwinds as reflected in Secretary Kerry's op-ed on 1 July 2014 in the Washington Post on where Iran needs to be. Moreover, as the Iranian Ambassador's recent letter to the IAEA demonstrates,[5] Iran continues to challenge, inter alia, the Agency's right and obligation to verify the correctness and completeness of Iran's declarations under the CSA, the legality of the IAEA Board resolutions, and the IAEA Secretariat's practices in reporting its findings in its reports to the IAEA Board and the U.N. Security Council.

Due to the fact that Iran has been running parts of its nuclear first clandestinely and then without satisfactorily fulfilling its reporting obligations to the IAEA and disregarding U.N. Security Council resolutions, the onus of proof bears heavily on Iran to show that its nuclear program is entirely peaceful.

I have recently published with David Albright and Andrea Stricker [6] an analysis on principles, which the negotiators crafting the comprehensive final agreement should follow. Five fundamental principles are:

1. Stable provisions;
2. A nuclear program meeting Iran's practical needs;
3. Effective verification;
4. Adequate irreversibility of constrains, and
5. Sufficient response time in case of violations.

In the following I will highlight some details that should be included to a final agreement negotiated. I will note a need for possible additional U.N. Security Council resolutions, and points to bear in mind on future reporting of the IAEA on safeguards implementation in Iran.

STABLE PROVISIONS

It is important for the credibility and durability of an agreement that it is crafted to minimize opportunities for violations and delays to achieve compliance.

The first requirement is that Iran provides a complete declaration of its past and current nuclear program as it did partially in 2003 when it started to implement the suspension agreement with the EU3. Such a declaration forms a clear-cut and essential baseline for the verification and monitoring activities by the IAEA.

Another important provision is the technical parameters of the nuclear program. An example of what would create an unstable and reversible situation that should be avoided is, for instance, suggestions that involve lowering the amount of enriched uranium Iran has access to while increasing the number of allowed centrifuges to 10,000 or more IR–1 centrifuges in order to increase breakout times. The instability arises from Iran continuing to make enriched uranium and maintaining residual stocks of enriched uranium to fuel research reactors. Keeping enriched uranium stocks exceedingly low would be impossible in practice. Practicalities of operating a centrifuge plant and a uranium conversion and fuel production complex would lead to larger enriched uranium stocks, compromising the original goal of longer breakout times. Such a proposal would require Iran to take actions almost monthly to keep its stocks below the agreed enriched uranium cap, something unlikely to be accomplished easily.

Our experiences from the implementation of the JPOA already demonstrate that stocks of low enriched uranium have grown due to logistical or operational difficulties. Any violation of the cap could be sudden and difficult to respond to. Regulating numbers of centrifuges is a far sounder approach than controlling enriched uranium stocks.

The third aspect to the stability equation is that by establishing a baseline, it also helps determine operating parameters. Experiences in implementing the various agreements with Iran since 2003 clearly demonstrate the importance of establishing unambiguous baselines for monitoring Iran's undertakings. Ambiguity in parameters (such as enrichment capacity, stocks of nuclear material, access to locations) leads to potential slippage. It is also necessary to specify explicit parameters for other fuel cycle facilities such as on laser enrichment. And it is important to include to the provisions that proscribed activities should not outsourced to other countries.

PRACTICAL NEEDS OF THE IRANIAN NUCLEAR PROGRAM

Limiting Iran's centrifuge program to say 2,000 to 4,000 IR–1 centrifuges is consistent with Iran's actual needs for enriched uranium for many years.[7] This number of centrifuges would provide Iran with sufficient enriched uranium for its existing research reactor programs and account for modest growth in them.

Besides breakout considerations, the simple fact for a smaller number of centrifuges is that Iran does not need to refuel the Bushehr reactor. Indeed, these limits would not allow for the fueling of the Bushehr nuclear power reactor. Recently, Iran's Supreme Leader in essence expressed this demand when he stated Iran requires enough centrifuges to produce about 190,000 kilograms of uranium hexafluoride separative work units per year (kg UF6 swu/year). In more standard units, this number would correspond to almost 130,000 kg U swu/year, which is equivalent to over 130,000 IR–1 centrifuges.

Iran's position of needing to produce its own fuel has to be measured against the realities that demonstrate why it in fact should not. Without extensive outside assistance in the form of key equipment, raw materials and advanced technology, Iran has limited prospect of actually building so many IR–1 centrifuges or an equivalent number of advanced centrifuges to fuel the Bushehr reactor over the next decade or two. It will need to continue relying on importing fuel from Russia or another major supplier. We also need to keep in mind that Iran has not demonstrated an ability to produce fuel of sufficient quality for the Bushehr nuclear power reactor, a key safety issue.

Moreover, Russia has not welcomed the idea of Iranian produced fuel in the Bushehr reactor. Russian concerns arise from the fact that having potentially defective Iranian fuel inserted into the Bushehr reactor, and fears of an accident which it, as the reactor supplier, could be held liable for. Such an events will also lead to reputational damage of Russian reactors.

EFFECTIVE VERIFICATION

Effective verification is an important core principle, but there are several challenges to overcome. Timely detection and prevention of the development and acquisition of nuclear weapons or a state's capability to produce them is a complex task. Development of weapons of mass destruction is one of the closest kept secrets of a state. There are things, which we know, and there are aspects of such programs, which we can perhaps to certain degree deduce, but also features, which we do not know.

In addition, Iran has refused to make concessions in this area. The IAEA must provide prompt warning of violations, determine the correctness and completeness of Iran's declarations, establish the total number of centrifuges produced by Iran and the size of its natural and enriched uranium stocks, and establish confidence in the absence of undeclared nuclear activities or facilities, including providing assurances on the absence of nuclear weapons related activities in Iran.

The strength of the IAEA verification system is access to nuclear material, facilities, equipment and people. To this end, the IAEA has, under its Comprehensive Safeguards Agreement (CSA) and Additional Protocol (AP), significant tools available if fully implemented and utilized. Iran argues that ratifying the Additional Protocol is enough but while such a step is welcome, it is not sufficient. The long-term agreement must also establish a range of other verification provisions, which collectively are often known as Additional Protocol Plus.

Throughout the long history of discussions on the scope and content of its nuclear program, Iran has often offered ''transparency'' to build international confidence on its nuclear program. Recently President Rouhani has again publicly stated Iran's readiness for greater transparency. More importantly, such transparency should be understood and implemented in a meaningful and systematic way. Even in the name of ''transparency,'' where Iran decides to ''show'' a place previously off limits (imposed by Iran), such inspection visits can have meaning only if substantially new information and discussions take place, and explanations are provided on the scope and content of the nuclear program. Hence openness should be clearly defined and become a legally binding undertaking, and not treated as good will visits to be granted when problems arise.

To minimize further the effects of the unknowns, it is important to understand the historical production and acquisition of uranium and its compounds by Iran. As part of the information obtained from the Iranian mines and milling facilities under the Framework for Cooperation,[8] Iran has provided information on uranium production of mines in Gcchine and Ardakan. It is important that the IAEA shares those actual numbers, and whereabouts of those materials with its member states, which may have additional information to complement the statements made by Iran.[9] This would also provide the member states indications on Iran's compliance with its undertakings. Releasing of such information by the IAEA will not jeopardize its independent assessment of Iran's declarations, but will complement information available.

Going further, according to the provisions of the CSA, a state has to declare all nuclear material in its territory. Thus military sites do not form sanctuaries, but the IAEA has right to conduct inspections on those under a CSA and complementary access under an AP, when appropriate. Iran has to provide the IAEA with unconditional and unrestricted access [10] to any and all areas, facilities, equipment, records, people, materials including source materials, which are deemed necessary by the IAEA to fulfill its requirements under the safeguards agreement, and to verify the correctness and completeness of Iran's declarations. These are needed both to understand the scope of the nuclear program as well as address the possible military dimensions (or PMD) aspects.

Accomplishing adequate verification, including the IAEA establishing that Iran's program is exclusively peaceful, will take many years. Just as an example, it took to the IAEA for medium size nuclear programs in European countries with CSA and AP implemented, about 5 years to conclude that all nuclear material in these countries was in peaceful use. Duration of an agreement for 20 years is reasonable in light of the two decades of Iran's noncompliance with its safeguards obligations and noncooperation with the IAEA.

A comprehensive agreement should also take the opportunity to assess the usefulness of strengthening certain linkages. For instance, the Sanctions Committee on Iran that was established under UNSC's Resolution 1737 [11] is a separately run mechanism from the IAEA verification process. At a minimum, these two bodies could be allowed to share information. It might also be reasonable to consider whether monitoring the implementation of sanctions should be assigned to a special unit to be established within the IAEA.

Adequate verification also requires Iran to verifiably stop its efforts to procure key proliferation-sensitive goods illegally for its nuclear programs. If not stopped, Iran could secretly purchase the wherewithal for secret nuclear sites or activities. This requires a continuation of national and United Nation Security Council sanctions on proliferation sensitive goods for the long term. However, an agreement will need to eventually allow for monitored Iranian purchases for its legitimate nuclear programs and civilian industries while ensuring that Iran is not buying goods illegally for banned activities.

Another important factor are the financial and human resources of the IAEA. In order to meet the verification requirements, the IAEA needs additional expertise on sensitive technologies. The arrangements have to be made that this staff has also access to Iranian facilities and can participate to discussions with Iranian expertise. Such arrangements worked well in South Africa and Libya, where the IAEA used its additional experts in addition to inspectors designated under the CSA.

To ensure that the IAEA gets the necessary legally binding authorities to conduct the additional verification work indicated in my statement, it is recommended that the U.N. Security Council endorse the agreement between P5+1 and Iran.

POSSIBLE MILITARY DIMENSIONS

Iran's most serious verification shortcoming remains its unwillingness to address the IAEA's concerns about the past and possibly on-going military dimensions of its nuclear programs. For the IAEA to conclude that all nuclear material is in peaceful use, this is not possible unless Iran satisfies the IAEA in this key area.

There are reports that much of the nuclear weapons related work by the military institutions came to halt in 2003. On the other hand, the IAEA has assessed in its reports that some of this R&D has continued since. It is important to understand the status of Iran's PMD efforts, noting that one of the last duties of Iranian personnel and organizations involved was to document work done. One plausible reason for such effort could have been to save information for further use. Unless properly addressed, it would be difficult to create a meaningful and robust verification regime for Iran. Such additional long-term monitoring took place in South Africa from 1993 until 2010 until the IAEA was able to conclude that all nuclear material in South Africa is in peaceful use. Otherwise, it would also render difficult for the IAEA to determine with confidence that any nuclear weapons activities are not ongoing—a necessary ingredient for a long-term deal.

The list of IAEA questions on the PMD is long. While the recent Framework for Cooperation agreements between Iran and the IAEA are welcome, the process is far from over. Many of the issues on the list above are interconnected, and they cannot be solved in isolation and not through the step-by-step process. In other words, there should be an understanding and actions provided by Iran that allows the IAEA to address the whole picture of the military dimension concerns. That should be an unambiguous condition to achieving a final accord that is meaningful in safeguards terms.

The agreement should also have provisions to ensure that Iran will decommission, dismantle or convert to nonnuclear or peaceful use in a verifiable and irreversible manner nuclear related equipment, materials, facilities and sites that contradict the provisions of the safeguards agreement or the spirit of Article III of the NPT. Such installations will be subject to a long-term monitoring by the IAEA.

Finally, limiting nuclear capabilities at known sites does not make sense if at the same time the deal makes it easier for Iran to make weapon-grade uranium at military sites. The comprehensive agreement must focus on both potential pathways as necessary for adequate verification to be carried out.

IRREVERSIBILITY

Irreversibility is understood as accepting that perfect irreversibility may not be possible but in practice recognizes that the restoration of the previous, unconstrained situation should take a long time—on order of years and not months. In the case of Iran, a long-term agreement would have little lasting value if Iran can reverse the constraints in a matter of days or months. The case of North Korea contains many examples where nuclear constraints imposed on reprocessing and the operation of the 5 MWe reactor were quickly undone and Pyongyang resumed its production of nuclear materials for nuclear weapons. This case also contains important examples of North Korea being unable to establish previous levels of plutonium production when an agreement ended. North Korea shut down its large gas-graphite reactors, ending their ability to make large amounts of weapon-grade plutonium, as a result of the 1994 U.S./DPRK Agreed Framework. When this agreement ended suddenly in 2002, North Korea was able to reestablish its small plutonium production capability. After 2009, North has put the reactor again in operation after reconstruction of the cooling system for the reactor.

Irreversibility is at the heart of the dispute about Iran limiting plutonium production in the Arak nuclear reactor. As a heavy water reactor Arak with its design can relatively easily make weapon-grade plutonium at a production rate sufficient to make enough weapon-grade plutonium up to two nuclear weapons per year. Iran has suggested reducing plutonium production in this reactor by using enriched uranium rather than natural uranium; other analysts have suggested in addition lowering the power of the reactor. It is true that combined, these proposals would reduce plutonium production to a fraction of the current value. However, both of these steps are reversible and Iran could in a straightforward, quick manner turn back the clock to a reactor able to make significant amounts of weapon-grade plutonium. The simple fix is for Iran to remove the currently installed core and replace it with a smaller one not able to hold enough natural uranium for the reactor to work. Iran so far resists this proposal.

With the above changes to the Arak reactor, there would also be no need for heavy water production—regular, ''light'' water could be used instead in this reactor. The heavy water could be shipped out and sold on the international market. This step would further make the Arak reactor changes reasonably irreversible.

Iran has also resisted making concessions about what to do with the centrifuges that would exceed a cap on the total agreed upon number of installed centrifuges. If the cap is say 4,000 IR–1 centrifuges, Iran would need to remove and render harmless almost 15,000 centrifuges installed in its Natanz and Fordow enrichment plants. If left installed, Iran could within months reconstitute operations and create a sizeable breakout capability. Thus, any proposal to keep excess centrifuges at the centrifuge plants is highly reversible and allows a quick reconstitution of dangerously unstable breakout times.

ADEQUATE RESPONSE TIME

An agreement must provide sufficient time to mount an effective response to major violations by Iran. There are two parts to this principle—one involves intrusive and effective IAEA inspections able to promptly detect and report noncompliance and the other recognizes that even the most intrusive inspections are alone inadequate to provide enough response time in the case of Iran. The latter's adequate response time requires significant limitations on content and parameters of Iran's nuclear programs and translates into a need to limit Iran's pathways to making nuclear weapons.

IAEA reports form a key part of the monitoring of compliance from the point of view of P5+1 and the international community. The member states can use these reports to complement their findings from their activities conducted by national means. From a practical point of view, the quarterly reporting on progress and findings by the IAEA should be sufficient. However, the IAEA should consider releasing factual information as it becomes available. Timeliness of conclusions depends on several parameters. This would entail the detection of the event, asking the clarification, additional sampling.

Much of that depends on the cooperation of the inspected party, but also on the event itself. While diversion of declared material is easily detectable, some more sophisticated events may take longer to detect. The IAEA's practice is to review each finding and claim meticulously, spending a fair amount of time and resources to refute or confirm any claim. Revised explanations provided by the inspected state also slow down the IAEA. This process needs to be re-thought. The IAEA verification system has its technical limitations. One of the tools the IAEA uses is environmental sampling, which has resulted in long in-between lead times. The latest IAEA report to its Board of Governors indicated that the environmental sample analysis results for Natanz FPEP, FEP, and Fordow were 28 January 2014, 5 February 2014, and 28 January 2014, respectively.[12] If additional samples and clarifications are required, the results will in practice take 6 months. The IAEA work process needs to be factored into an overall understanding of timeliness of response.

An effective metric of adequate limits on Iran's main overt pathway to nuclear weapons, its centrifuge program, is breakout time, which measures the length of time Iran would need to produce enough weapon-grade uranium for a single nuclear weapon. This technical breakout value is converted via detailed breakout calculations into an equivalent number of centrifuges that would be installed in Iran, which results in an oft-stated limit of about 2,000–4,000 IR–1 centrifuges remaining in Iran as part of a comprehensive deal.

There are other reasons to make known breakout times longer. In the past, Iran has conducted activities, and concealed them in such ways that were not quickly detected or stalled in letting the IAEA to proceed with its investigations. Achieving the necessary evidence to judge with high confidence that violations have indeed occurred is time consuming and intelligence reliant in key cases, such as the discovery of the once-covert Natanz and Fordow Fuel Enrichment Plants, clandestine centrifuge R&D at Kalaye Electric, black market nuclear related imports including imports of nuclear material, some with possible military uses.

There is also the still unresolved file on the development of nuclear weapons. The IAEA has not yet been able to verify that Iran has submitted all its nuclear material to the IAEA safeguards. We do not also know how many centrifuges Iran has manufactured and where they are today. Moreover, a larger program also makes it easier for Iran to hide illicit foreign procurements, some of which could be slated for a clandestine program. To this end, it is also important—as mentioned in my testimony on 10 June 2014—that Iran has to report all imports and manufacturing of single and dual use items regardless whether the end user is the nuclear program and provides the IAEA access to that information and items.[13]

While breakout time does not include the total time to produce a nuclear weapon for testing underground or mounting on a missile, the production of the weapon-grade uranium is the more difficult and time consuming portion of making a nuclear weapon. Once Iran has enough weapon-grade uranium for a weapon, the material would ostensibly vanish to covert sites for further weaponization efforts, which could be small in size without visible detectable signatures as it was in the case of South Africa. Additional concerns are the facts that Iran may have received sufficient amount of design information to avoid testing. If a gun-type nuclear device is a goal, it requires more material, but there is no need for testing. Thus, the priority must be to limit Iran's ability to first produce the weapon-grade uranium.

IN SUMMARY

The actual verification process will be time consuming and will stretch over many years, especially more so for a nuclear program in Iran that had been largely clandestine in nature, broad and complex. Forthcoming and proper cooperation from Iran could set the tone for the country to have in place a limited nuclear program. A meaningful and robust verification system with the requisite elements is needed to support a long-term deal.

End Notes

[1] Communication dated 27 November 2013 received from the EU High Representative Concerning the text of the Joint Plan of Action, IAEA, INFCIRC/855, 27 November 2013.

[2] United Nations Security Council Resolution 1929, 9 June 2010.

[3] The involvement of military institutes includes support to the acquisition of nuclear technology, building the nuclear infrastructure, and work related to acquisition of nuclear materials, nuclear source materials, and key raw materials, and production of single use nuclear equipment. Of concern is also work by these organizations related to neutron physics, neutron sources, high explosives, missile re-entry vehicle, which appear to have the characteristic of nuclear weapon development.

[4] Joint Statement on a Framework for Cooperation, GOV/INF/2013/14, IAEA, 11 November 2013.

[5] Communication dated 4 June 2014 received from the Permanent Mission of the Islamic Republic of Iran to the Agency regarding the Report of the Director General on the Implementation of Safeguards in Iran, IAEA, INFCIRC/866, 13 June 2014.

[6] D. Albright, O. Heinonen, and A. Stricker, "The Six's" Guiding Principles in Negotiating with Iran, ISIS, 3 June 2014.

[7] Defining Iranian Nuclear Programs in a Comprehensive Solution under the Joint Plan of Action, ISIS, 15 January 2014.

[8] Implementation of the NPT Safeguards Agreement and relevant provisions of Security Council Resolutions in the Islamic Republic Iran, GOV/2014/28, paras 7–8, IAEA, 23 May 2014.

[9] Recent IAEA reports have acknowledged the receipt of such information, but no quantities have been shared with the member states in written reports.

[10] Due to the nature of the verification and monitoring such access should be done in short notice at, inter alia, centrifuge assembly and component manufacturing plants and at enrichment facilities.

[11] United Nations Security Council Resolution 1737, 23 December 2006.

[12] IAEA, "Implementation of the NPT Safeguards Agreement and Relevant Provisions of Security Council Resolutions in the Islamic Republic of Iran," GOV/2014/28, 22 May 2014.

[13] Olli Heinonen, Testimony on "Verifying Iran's Nuclear Compliance," The United States House Committee on Foreign Affairs, 10 June 2014.

The CHAIRMAN. Thank you.

Mr. Singh.

STATEMENT OF MICHAEL SINGH, LANE–SWIG SENIOR FELLOW AND MANAGING DIRECTOR, THE WASHINGTON INSTITUTE, WASHINGTON, DC

Mr. SINGH. Chairman Menendez and Ranking Member Corker, thanks for this opportunity to address the committee.

I am a strong supporter of a diplomatic resolution to the Iran nuclear crisis and I have been involved with the P5+1 talks since their inception. I am concerned, though, that we are not close to a true diplomatic resolution, that in fact if we have a deal it is likely to be one which in fact postpones a real diplomatic resolution and weakens our ability to achieve such a resolution.

If we have a deal in this next 4-month period, I am concerned that it is going to be one which falls short of what should be our minimum requirements. It is not likely to require Iran to dismantle anything, including those facilities that it built illegally in violation of NPT requirements. It would, in fact, probably permit Iran to engage in more nuclear activity than it engages in today under the JPOA. It probably will not require Iran to come clean on its past weaponization activities or give inspectors access to military sites, as Dr. Heinonen said. It will not deal most likely with ballistic missiles, which are such a vexing threat in places like East Asia, as we have seen in other reports. And it would allow Iran in a matter of years to be free of any constraints whatsoever on its nuclear program.

What we get in exchange for this deal is a commitment by Iran not to build nuclear weapons. But of course, the very reason we are engaged in this process is that Iran has violated similar commitments in the past.

We would also get enhanced inspections, but I do think that we are placing too much stock in what inspections can actually achieve, because they would be hampered by, first, just the sheer size of Iran's nuclear program that we would leave in place under such a deal, and by Iran's refusal to come clean on its past work, as Dr. Heinonen said, and frankly the absence of a clear willingness on the part of the United States or the international community to enforce those inspection requirements. I think that the larger the nuclear program we leave in place, the less likely the international community is going to be to punish incremental cheating on those obligations.

The Iranian regime, as both of you know, plays a major role in destabilizing the Middle East and supporting terrorism. Frankly, the arms embargo that is in place against Iran, which would address for example its provision of rockets to groups like Hamas, that comes from Resolution 1747, which is a nuclear resolution, which could get lifted as part of a deal.

This sort of deal that we are talking about would leave tremendous nuclear capabilities in the hands of that regime and embolden and enrich that regime. It would also have other negative implications for American interests. It would give other states in the region an incentive to match Iran's nuclear capabilities. It would undermine our nonproliferation efforts globally and encourage the spread of that enrichment and reprocessing technology to other places. And, frankly, it would damage our own influence and prestige; they are already pretty damaged, and this is the issue upon which those things will be most judged in the Middle East.

How have we reached the juncture that we are at right now? Well, if you look at the JPOA, in exchange for temporary, reversible steps by Iran we made major concessions that the Iranians have been seeking for a long time: that it could enrich uranium indefinitely and that any constraints on it would be in any case temporary.

We have this saying that nothing is agreed until anything is agreed. Things are more complicated than that. It will be very difficult to take back these concessions. I think the Iranians will seek to pocket these and use them as a baseline for any future negotiations.

We also, frankly, have not put forward a threatening alternative to an agreement, which I think has led Iran to reject even very generous offers. Our sanctions threat has been undermined and we have not responded to that increase in oil exports that we were talking about earlier. Our military threat has been undermined because of the paralyzed indecision with which we have faced situations in Syria, Iraq, Ukraine, and elsewhere.

And it was an error for us to stray from what had been our previous approach, which was dismantling for dismantling: Iran dismantles those illegal nuclear facilities in exchange for the dismantling of sanctions against it. Iran and frankly sometimes our own officials have portrayed that approach as maximalist, but I do not think it is maximalist. In fact it is reasonable, because Iran, as was stated before, has no need for those fuel cycle activities which we are asking it to forgo, but it does have a need for sanctions relief, a deep need for sanctions relief.

We should be prepared, and we are prepared, to accept a civilian nuclear program in Iran, on the condition that Iran import its nuclear fuel, as most countries in the world, including the United States, do.

I think the only scenario in which we should be prepared to live with a significant Iranian nuclear capability is one in which we see evidence of a broader strategic shift by Iran, and it is clearly not in evidence today, given Iran's support for terrorism and its refusal to even be transparent with us about what it has done on the nuclear issue in the past.

The most important question for policymakers now is how to make a good deal, one which advances U.S. interests, more likely. We need to not only adopt a firmer line in these talks, but we need to enhance our leverage by making those alternatives to a deal look worse.

We can do that in a couple if different ways. We can strengthen our sanctions threat, first by a unified message from the White

House and Congress that, yes, more sanctions will follow an agreement. I think action on that is required now.

We need to act more energetically in response to those, what appear to be dissipation, as some of the members said, of the sanctions and the increase in the oil exports in particular. We can strengthen our military threat, which is also critical here, by sending clear messages about our enduring commitment to this region and then backing up that message with adequate defense and diplomatic and intelligence resources, by taking firmer steps to counter Iranian support for terrorism—the provision of rockets to Gaza and things like that—to counter the impression that Iran gets a free pass as long as these talks are going on. And we can try to strengthen our weakened alliances in the region, which have really withered to a point we should not have let them reach.

So to conclude, I worry that we have become captive to a false choice between a flawed deal and the prospect of a military conflict. I reject that false choice. I think our true choice is between a deal which will set back our interests and a firmer approach to diplomacy which holds out hope of advancing those interests.

Thank you very much.

[The prepared statement of Mr. Singh follows:]

Prepared Statement of Michael Singh

Chairman Menendez, Ranking Member Corker, and members of the committee, thank you for inviting me to discuss the United States diplomatic efforts to end the threat posed by Iran's nuclear ambitions. I have closely followed the P5+1 talks since their inception—first as an aide to the Secretary of State, then as the official responsible for Iran at the National Security Council, and now as a research scholar—and while I strongly support a diplomatic resolution to the Iran nuclear crisis, I am concerned at the juncture at which we now find ourselves.

Our negotiators' mantra with regard to these negotiations is, as it should be, that "no deal is better than a bad deal." But how can one tell a good deal from a bad deal, from the point of view of the United States?

- A good deal is one which clearly advances American interests—not only our interest in nuclear nonproliferation globally, but in the stability of the Middle East and our prestige and influence in that region, which has in recent years declined sharply.
- The talks are a diplomatic effort to address the grave threat to our interests—shared with our allies in the region and beyond—posed by Iranian nuclear efforts.
- As in any negotiation, any agreement must also be acceptable to Iran; but whether any particular deal is acceptable to Iran depends not only on the content of that deal but on whether Iranian authorities believe the alternatives to the deal would be worse.

Our negotiators appear to be on the cusp of a historic deal with the Iranian regime. Whether that deal is a historic accomplishment or a historic error, however, depends on whether it durably ensures that Iran is prevented from acquiring nuclear weapons and advances our interests in the region broadly, or whether it leaves the region less stable, our allies less confident in our resolve, and Iran with sufficient residual nuclear capacity to develop nuclear weapons in the near future.

Status of Commitments Under the "Joint Plan of Action"

On the surface, the interim agreement or "Joint Plan of Action" (JPOA) between Iran and the P5+1 has largely performed as advertised.

- On July 20, the International Atomic Energy Agency reported that Iran has met its commitments under the JPOA.
- The Obama administration has reported that the sanctions relief provided to Iran has remained at or under its initial estimate of $6–$7 billion.

However, some questions exist about both claims.

- The Bipartisan Policy Center reported that Iran has managed to increase the efficiency of its installed IR–1 centrifuges by 25 percent in the last 6 months.
- The Foundation for Defense of Democracies and Roubini Global Economics have placed the value of direct sanctions relief at $11 billion if condensate exports—not covered by sanctions—are accounted for, and indirect relief at an even higher figure depending on what portion of Iran's increased economic growth is attributable to a rise in consumer and business confidence stemming from the JPOA and sanctions relief.
- Iranian oil exports have steadily risen since the signing of the JPOA; they averaged 1.25 091.3 million barrels per day over the first 6 months of 2014 and currently stand at 1.4 million barrels per day.
- Much of this rise is attributable to an increase in Chinese oil imports from Iran, which averaged 627,742 barrels per day during the first 6 months of 2014, up 48 percent from the same period last year. This significant increase has not drawn a response from the United States as far as I am aware.
- It is important to note that even though oil export revenue is higher than anticipated, that revenue remains difficult for Iran to access due to the requirement it be placed in escrow.

It is important to bear in mind, however, that the JPOA did not address all of Iran's nuclear activities.

- The JPOA provided for a halt in the progress in certain activities, along with a reduction in Iran's level of enrichment and stockpile of 20-percent-enriched uranium, but it allowed other nuclear activities to continue apace.
- The agreement did not address two of the three elements of Iran's nuclear program—ballistic missiles and weaponization research (or "possible military dimensions" or PMD).
- Missiles have not been addressed at all, whereas the question of weaponization has been left with the IAEA, which has reported a disappointing lack of progress even as Iran has continued to deny inspectors access to the Parchin site while engaging in work there likely designed to obscure its past activities.
- Even the one element of Iran's nuclear effort addressed by the JPOA—fuel fabrication—was dealt with only partially, as Iran continues to stockpile more than enough enriched uranium for a nuclear weapon and to develop advanced centrifuges that if installed would reduce its breakout time further.

The JPOA "timeout" applied not only to Iranian nuclear progress, but also to Western economic pressure, the momentum of which had been building.

- For Iran, the JPOA provided a reprieve from what had been steadily mounting economic pressure. Per a study by my colleague, Dr. Patrick Clawson, at the Washington Institute for Near East Policy, Tehran for its part has used the "time and space" provided by the JPOA to make key macroeconomic adjustments—spending cuts, exchange rate adjustment, a tightening of monetary policy—to stabilize its economy.
- Clawson's study finds that these adjustments have decreased Iran's rate of inflation from over 40 percent in early 2013 to 17 percent today, and have put the country on track to achieve 1.5 percent GDP growth this year and 2.3 percent per year thereafter, even without sanctions relief.
- As such, Iran's current oil exports would easily provide sufficient foreign exchange to balance its current account were it able to access that revenue.

At a deeper level, the JPOA represented a significant diplomatic advance for Iran. In exchange for easily reversible and explicitly temporary pauses to selected nuclear activities, Iran obtained concessions from the United States which it had sought since the beginning of this diplomatic process in 2003.

- The United States implicitly renounced the requirement—enshrined in multiple U.N. Security Council resolutions whose legitimacy Iran had denounced—that Iran suspend enrichment, reprocessing, and heavy water-related activities, and gained American acknowledgement that Iran would continue to enrich uranium indefinitely.
- Furthermore, it secured legitimacy for its facilities at Natanz and Arak, which had been constructed secretly and in violation of Iran's Nonproliferation Treaty obligations.
- Finally, it established that any limitations on Iranian nuclear activities—short of the actual construction of a nuclear weapon—would be temporary.

PROGRESS OF NEGOTIATIONS UNDER THE JPOA

The JPOA represented a shift in the underlying negotiating framework from addressing Iran's violations to addressing its purported "practical needs" for nuclear fuel cycle activities.

- Previously the U.N. Security Council had required that Iran suspend all such activities, leaving open the question of whether and when they would be permitted to resume.
- This position was reversed by Obama administration officials, who termed it "maximalist" or, in the words of then-Senator John Kerry in 2009, "ridiculous."
- Yet it was neither—the P5+1 had been prepared to offer Iran not only sanctions relief but a long list of other incentives in exchange for Iranian agreement to halt its nuclear activities. In other words, we offered Iran something which it needed desperately in exchange for something it did not, if its claims to eschew nuclear weapons are true.
- For Tehran to have turned down this offer—as well as more recent offers conceding significant fuel cycle activities—suggests that it values those activities more than economic relief, which is hardly a sensible position for a country blessed with abundant fossil fuel reserves, and which in any event has been offered the opportunity to obtain nuclear fuel through import like nearly every other country with nuclear power.
- It is this Iranian position—not the P5+1 requirement that Iran suspend fuel cycle activities—that is unreasonable. Yet by not challenging it, we have found ourselves tactically on our heels.
- Having won this ground, Iran staked out a truly maximalist position—that it required not just the 19,000 centrifuges it possessed as the talks began, but an additional 100,000 centrifuges or more.
- As a result, it is able to portray, however cynically, its most recent offer to simply maintain its current centrifuge stocks in exchange for sanctions relief as a significant compromise.

Since its signing, there have been few signs that the JPOA is leading to an agreement that will advance American interests.

- The United States has significantly reduced its long-standing demands of Iran. In addition to the major concessions made merely to obtain the JPOA, the United States reportedly made others, including that Iran's Arak research reactor could remain a plutonium-producing heavy water reactor, albeit with modifications, and that the Fordow enrichment facility need not be closed.
- In addition, there are few signs that weaponization research or missiles will be specifically addressed in a deal.
- The major constraints on Iran in a deal will likely be on its number and type of centrifuges, its level of uranium enrichment and plutonium production, and the size and composition of its enriched uranium stockpile. Iran will also be required to accept enhanced inspections.
- These are important issues, to be sure, but the restrictions will in any event be temporary. There is as yet no indication that Iran will be required to dismantle or ship out any part of its nuclear infrastructure.
- Thus, an agreement will neither be comprehensive—even with respect to nuclear issues—nor final, but will likely permit Iran greater nuclear activities than it conducts under the JPOA.
- Rather than requiring that Iran dismantle its nuclear program in exchange for the dismantling of sanctions, we are seemingly poised to alleviate the pressure on Iran in exchange for its promise to temporarily halt the expansion of the program it has already built in defiance of its international obligations.

Successful negotiation depends not just on how each party values a particular deal, but whether it deems the alternatives to a negotiated agreement as better or worse for its interests. We have not persuaded Tehran that the alternative to a deal would be damaging to Iranian interests.

- Iran likely perceives that the two most threatened alternatives to a diplomatic settlement—additional sanctions or a military strike—have become less threatening since the signing of the JPOA.
- Persuading oil importers such as China—whose oil imports from Iran, as I have already noted, have been rising during the past 6 months despite sanctions without attracting any American response—would be difficult absent a clear demonstration of U.S. will, especially if Iran does not significantly ramp up its nuclear activities upon the collapse of talks.

- American military credibility, already undermined by our failure to enforce the President's declared redline on Syria, has suffered further as we have greeted crises in Iraq, Ukraine, and the South China Sea with paralyzed indecision.

In sum, the United States begins the next 4 months of talks at a significant disadvantage.

- Iran has already extracted valuable concessions from the P5+1, which Tehran will seek to pocket and establish as a new baseline for any future diplomacy.
- Even as the value to Iran of a diplomatic settlement has declined, the prospect and cost of the threatened alternatives have as well, reducing Iran's incentive to accept even generous offers.
- Those generous offers might be warranted were there evidence that Iran were undergoing the sort of ''strategic shift'' we have long sought; but Iran's support for terrorism, destabilizing regional activities, and anti-American vitriol continue unabated.
- In this context, a narrow deal that leaves Iran with significant residual nuclear weapons capability would set back American interests rather than advance them.
- The urgent task before American policymakers, if they are to achieve a worthwhile diplomatic solution to the Iran nuclear crisis, is to alter this equation.

THE WAY AHEAD

The fundamental bargain between the United States and Iran should be dismantling for dismantling—Iran dismantles its illicit nuclear infrastructure in exchange for the dismantling of nuclear sanctions.

- The U.S. should remain prepared to accept a civilian nuclear power program in Iran, but one which depends on imported fuel; the U.S. should not accept indigenous fuel cycle activities in Iran until it has established its peaceful intent.
- Congress should insist that nuclear facilities built in violation of Iran's NPT obligations be dismantled; this is important not only for regional stability, but for the integrity of the nonproliferation regime globally.
- Iran will portray these terms as overly harsh, but in fact they impose no hardship on Iran's economy or its people; on the contrary, Iran would enjoy a civilian nuclear program that operates similarly to those in many other countries, including the United States, and much-needed economic relief.

The alternative—permitting Iran a large nuclear infrastructure—strikes me as imprudent and unlikely to succeed in the face of Iranian determination to advance its nuclear weapons capability.

- The success of any deal which leaves Iran with a large residual nuclear capability would depend first on the extent and intrusiveness of inspections.
- Yet those inspections will be hampered by the size of Iran's nuclear program, its refusal thus far to come clean on past nuclear activities and thus provide inspectors with a ''roadmap,'' and by hesitancy to grant inspectors access to military facilities such as Parchin, which are likely as vital to Iranian nuclear efforts as declared civilian facilities.
- Those same factors would decrease the likelihood of detecting covert nuclear facilities, which is important given that the intelligence community judges that Iran is likely to use such facilities, not its declared sites, if it chooses to make a nuclear weapon.
- The success of a deal would further depend on whether the consequences for Iran of cheating are sufficiently severe, which in turn depends on our and our allies' willingness and ability to enforce the deal.
- Because re-imposing sanctions could be a slow and uncertain process, in the event of Iranian cheating Washington would likely be left with an unpalatable choice between mere diplomatic reprimands and military action. It is important that we act prudently now to avoid finding ourselves in such a corner in the future.

A deal of this sort would have potentially negative implications for U.S. interests in the Middle East and beyond.

- It would embolden and enrich a regime which has demonstrated a willingness to support virtually any group or cause which is opposed to U.S. interests.
- It would lend credence to Iranian efforts to portray the United States as irresolute and unreliable, and to call into question the legitimacy of the U.N. Security Council.

- It could lead U.S. allies in the region to seek to match Iranian nuclear capabilities, and to counter Iranian activities in the region without coordinating with the United States.
- Finally, it would undermine U.S. efforts to limit the spread of enrichment and reprocessing technologies globally, which are inherently dual-use in nature.

Thus the sort of deal the P5+1 has offered—permitting Iran a bounded residual nuclear capacity in exchange for enhanced inspections—should only be contemplated if we see evidence that Iran is undertaking a broader strategic shift.

- While offering no guarantee of success, evidence of such a shift would provide confidence that Iran would be committed to upholding a deal rather than determined to evade its constraints or exploit its loopholes.
- Examples of such evidence would be willingness by Iran to come clean on its past nuclear activities, and to curtail destabilizing activities such as support for terrorism and the provision of arms to proxy militias.
- Such steps should be considered as conditions for any final sanctions relief. This would also hold benefits for Iran, as it would hold out the prospect of normalized relations with the international community and the lifting not just of nuclear sanctions, but sanctions more broadly.
- Given that these issues are unlikely to be addressed in the current negotiations, and the importance of seeing evidence that Iran is complying with an agreement before irreversibly alleviating pressure, any sanctions relief should be back-loaded.

Success in the negotiations depends on more than just the content of our offers—it depends on increasing the credibility of our threatened alternatives to an agreement. If Iran's alternatives look worse, it is more likely to accept a negotiated agreement.

- The threat of sanctions can be made more credible via a unified message from the White House and Congress that pressure will be increased if talks do not succeed by November 24.
- Sanctions can also be strengthened by responding with greater alacrity to the increase in Iranian oil exports.
- Our military credibility can be enhanced by making clear our continuing commitment to the Middle East through messaging—particularly by making clear that the "rebalance" to Asia and our pursuit of energy "independence" do not portend a retreat from the region—and backing up that commitment with adequate military and diplomatic resources and by seeking to strengthen our seriously weakened alliance system in the region.
- Our military credibility can also be strengthened by responding more vigorously to other threats to regional stability, particularly in Iraq and Syria, and by taking additional steps to counter destabilizing Iranian policies, particularly its provision of arms to groups such as Hezbollah, Hamas, and Palestinian Islamic Jihad.
- Finally, Congress and the administration should jointly ensure that, whether or not a deal is reached with Iran, we continue to devote adequate intelligence and diplomatic resources to monitoring and responding to Iranian activities; we cannot afford to shift those resources elsewhere in the belief that, in the wake of a deal, we can move on to other problems.

Achieving a nuclear agreement that adequately secures our interests and those of our allies will be difficult and require patience, and taking steps to reassert our commitment to the Middle East, reassure allies, and deter Iran will require effort and resources when other crises around the world are competing for both. But these two broad lines of action can be mutually reinforcing—Iran is more likely to accept and adhere to a stringent nuclear accord if it perceives that the U.S. is willing to hold out at the negotiating table and is not looking for a quick exit from the region, and any adverse regional consequences of an agreement may be less if it is perceived to reflect American resolve rather than diffidence. To state that "no deal is better than a bad deal" is only meaningful given some yardstick for what makes a deal "good" or "bad"; for the United States, that yardstick must be the extent to which a deal advances our—and our allies'—strategic interests in the Middle East and beyond.

The CHAIRMAN. Thank you both for your testimony. You bring up some very important points.

Dr. Heinonen, you wrote in an article recently that, "Negotiations in Vienna have shown that the principles driving the positions of the P5+1 are markedly different than those of Iran." Can you explain the two sets of principles you are referring to, behind the P5+1 and the Iranian positions, and why those two different sets of positions make it more difficult to reach an agreement?

Dr. HEINONEN. I think if we look at the history of the last 11 years—these negotiations have been going 11 years; really, this is a story of now 4,000 nights and not 1,000 nights—and you look at what has been the driving force in Iran, they want to maintain and save their nuclear program in the format what it is today, which will include uranium enrichment and it will probably include also the capability to produce plutonium in a heavy water reactor.

This has been all along there, through these hardships. You read the statements made by Mr. Rouhani in 2005 when he left office, how he explained how he was able under those difficult circumstances to preserve the enrichment program by suspending it for a while and how he was able to rescue the uranium conversion program.

And then we look to the talks of today. When the Supreme Leader says that we want to have 190,000 centrifuges and produce uranium fuel for Bushehr reactor, it is clear that the bottom line is the enrichment program has to survive.

Then you look which are the challenges Iran is facing if they want to produce that nuclear fuel. The first thing is the mere fact, actually they do not have enough uranium in their soil to support such a program. So what good is then for you if you are able to do enrichment if you cannot find the soil from your own—uranium from your own soil?

Then when you look at this one, look at the fuel manufacturing technology which they do not yet have, the sole reason is they want to preserve the enrichment program from, as some Senator said here before.

Then the other side of the gulf is that actually we do not want to have any enrichment program with Iran because of a number of reasons. So I think this is what I meant in this writing. This is a very different starting point and, unfortunately, now the situation is that the spiritual leader went and said it is 190,000. It is a great number, a big number.

The CHAIRMAN. Let me ask you, what do you read into the letter—that I referenced before to Secretary Sherman that is in your testimony—by the Iranian Ambassador, questioning all of the IAEA's authorities in this regard?

Dr. HEINONEN. Well, this is——

The CHAIRMAN. Is it buying time? Is this extending the period? What do you think is the intent, from your experience at the IAEA?

Dr. HEINONEN. I think that this tells me that when the agreement will be there, whatever will be negotiated, now hopefully in the next few months, when it comes to the implementation then IAEA steps in and starts to talk with Iran how to do these things in practice. Since these are the same people who are part of the negotiations, they are still posturing the old language which was there. So the IAEA negotiations will start in headwinds and every action IAEA tries to take could be challenged by this thing of, okay, it is not within your legal authority to do this and this, and we will end up with these implementation problems.

The CHAIRMAN. So you are saying that, even presuming that the P5+1 negotiators can reach an agreement in 4 months, that then there will be a whole other set of negotiations with the IAEA as to how in fact those agreements will be enforced?

Dr. HEINONEN. Yes, this is the practice.

The CHAIRMAN. Let me ask you then, what lessons should we draw from the failure of the framework agreement with North Korea as we deal with this one?

Dr. HEINONEN. Yes, I was part of the IAEA side in 1994. I think that there are several lessons. The first thing which we learned here is exactly the same, challenging the authority of the IAEA. You remember that North Korea was about to leave the NPT and therefore they said that they are not bound with the provisions of the safeguards agreement and therefore the IAEA did not have any authority to do certain things, and they challenged every step in that process of what the IAEA did in practice.

I can give you an example. We were not even able to use the word ''inspection'' because ''inspection'' is in the safeguards agreement and therefore you cannot use it. I do not think Iran will take that line, but it will be an uphill battle. There will be headwinds, as we already see in the difference in views in the implementation of this framework of cooperation between Iran and IAEA. Very recently, Mr. Salehi challenged some of the statements and actions taken by IAEA with regard to the military dimension. It was a very different interpretation from the agency paper versus what Mr. Salehi said in public.

The CHAIRMAN. So when I hear Secretary Sherman say, well, they will have to satisfy the IAEA, that can be, based upon Iran's present status or actions, litigated for some time in terms of what the IAEA believes is appropriate for verification and enforcement on all the dimensions, including the possible weaponization elements, while the sanctions relief is suspended?

Dr. HEINONEN. I think this is a good remark. The only thing that I we say, that these provisions need to be enshrined to this agreement in such a way that it becomes legally binding and when one is not in compliance the noncompliance has consequences.

The CHAIRMAN. Let me ask you one final question from your experience at the IAEA. Is a good model the South African model, which ultimately admitted in 1993 to possessing a nuclear program with military dimensions, and then showed unprecedented cooperation by allowing anywhere, any time inspections? It took them 17 years to get a clean bill of health, but is something along those lines appropriate? I think that is probably less of a program than we are talking about in Iran, but what is your perceptions of that?

Dr. HEINONEN. It is less of a program, it was more of a program, because they had much more nuclear material which had not been declared before and there was a history of operation of enrichment for 20 years. One of the stumbling blocks was actually verification of the wastes. They were in 70,000 barrels and it took a long, long time just to go through those.

But why it was successful was that actually the government had changed their view. They had given up their nuclear weapons program. They wanted to close that chapter in the history of South Africa, and in order to do that they needed someone to certify that and that organization was the IAEA. So the cooperation was there. Once they did this disclosure in 1993, it was easy to go because the whole government was set up to help the IAEA to complete its mission.

But if that change does not take place in Iran, that they want to come—that they come clean, want to come clean from their past, it is going to be difficult, as it was in North Korea.

The CHAIRMAN. So even though in this case South Africa had determined as a government that it wanted to end that chapter in its history, wanted to end its nuclear program, it took 17 years to get a clean bill of health, with the government willing and wanting to end its nuclear program? I think that is pretty instructive as to when we say long-term verification and enforcement agreements, it is very different, the two paradigms here, between where Iran is at and where South Africa was at.

Senator Corker.

Senator CORKER. Thank you, Mr. Chairman, and thank you both for being here.

I listened, Mr. Heinonen, to some of the complications relative to having this negotiation after the fact. I know that is the way it has to occur, but I wondered. We keep pressing about the full transparency of what their program was about in the past and relative to what IAEA would be doing in the future, how important is that to understand fully what their program was in the past?

Dr. HEINONEN. You do not need to know every nut and bolt from the program, but you need to know how far they got, for two reasons. One reason is that it is a part of your risk assessment, how much unknowns you tolerate when you agree with the number of centrifuges, if you allow them to have a sort of breakout—certain centrifuges enrichment capability. That is one reason.

The second reason with your unknowns is that you certainly do not want to—you want to know how far they got and you want to see that they are not reconstituting the program. So therefore you need to know what was done, where it was done, and how it was done. This exactly took place in South Africa. Still in 2010 the IAEA inspectors visited some of the military sites to confirm that those actions are not reconstituted.

So I see it as a very important in setting the baseline so that a proper, robust, reliable monitoring scheme can be established.

Senator CORKER. When you do that, how do you know that, when people are sharing with you what they were doing in the past, how do you know that that is in reality what they were doing in the past?

Dr. HEINONEN. It is actually a number of things. We normally call it multielement analysis. You look what the people tell you, you look at the experiments they have been doing. Do they make sense, do they fit to the nuclear program at that point in time when they do those experiments? You can indirectly confirm it by seeing the equipment which they have both for that and some other events which have taken place.

So it is like a mosaic where you have bits and pieces all over and which then will have some gaps, but from that mosaic you can establish a relatively cohesive picture of what has been taking place. Then there should be no outliers and no inconsistencies.

Senator CORKER. One last question along those lines.

I think, especially with a country like Iran that has multiple silos and arrangements with entities that sometimes are part of government, sometimes are not, how do you know that there is not some clandestine program? The IAEA goes in, they inspect what we know of. How do you have assurances, especially with a country like Iran, that there are not some other activities that are taking place? And what kind of abilities does the organization have to actually figure that out?

Dr. HEINONEN. IAEA has its own authorities and its own practices and skills. But it heavily draws also from the support of the member states. Actually, this is the reason why I wrote in my testimony also that it is important that the IAEA reports in a very transparent way what they have seen, what they have been told, what is where, so that the member states can, which have their own national means to find some of those details or have formed their own picture about the nuclear program, can see is this consistent with what the IAEA sees and what Iran tells.

Therefore the reporting is the important thing, and that is why it disturbed me quite a lot when the Ambassador in his letter to Mr. Amano said that he does not like the way IAEA put some technical details to the report, because this is I think one of the keys to success of the IAEA. Only then IAEA can serve its member states if it has that information.

Senator CORKER. Mr. Singh, thank you. Thank you for your testimony and the answers.

The goalposts continue to move as we talk about where this deal is going. But I just want to give a hypothetical. Let us say that the administration ended up in a situation with 3,000 centrifuges, no Arak, no Fordow, and very extensive and intrusive inspections. How would that affect Iran's behavior in the region? How would that affect their ability in the future? How would it affect the neighborhood?

Mr. SINGH. Well, it is important to note first of all that that sort of deal does not seem to be in prospect, because on some of those issues you mentioned, Senator, we have already made significant concessions——

Senator CORKER. I appreciate your testimony, candidly, and feel very aligned with much of what you had to say. But let us just go back to, again, we have unfortunately seen the goalposts move, but let us just say that, hypothetically, that is where things ended up. Talk to me about the response?

Mr. SINGH. I think that a lot of it will depend upon not just the sort of particulars in the deal, but the context as well. Look, some of our allies are not happy with the concessions that we made. They would like us to have not made those concessions. But I think that if we had a sort of——

Senator CORKER. Some of our allies as part of the P5?

Mr. SINGH. That is a hard question to answer, because some of our allies in the P5+1 may not be happy with those, but they are unlikely to say that publicly. I think some of our allies in the region, both Israel and some of the Gulf States, have been more outspoken in the way they feel about that.

So the risk is to our position in the region, and how folks perceive the nature of the agreement. Therefore I think the context of our policy in the region is important to how allies and others will judge it. Do they view it as an expression of American resolve or do they view it as an expression of American weakness?

If we have the right policy context—what are we doing in Syria, what are we doing on Iraq, are we repairing our alliance system in the region—we can influence how folks see an agreement, and we can especially, very importantly, influence how they view our willingness to actually uphold an agreement.

In my view, our allies think that the concessions we have made on enrichment—conceding any number of centrifuges whatsoever to Iran—is not good to have conceded. They think that we should not have done that. That that is a view that is widely shared in the region.

But again, the context is very important and so to improve that situation, to improve how it is perceived, there are certain steps we can take.

Senator CORKER. This is the last question I will have. You alluded to the fact that we started off in a not great place, and I think people on both sides of the aisle here are concerned about where we began. But you said in your testimony that you felt like we could get to a good end still. So with where we began and where we are, how would you go about doing that?

Mr. SINGH. Look, I think that the reality is we are where we are in the negotiations, and so the question before us here is how do we take the situation and make a good deal out of it, make the best situation out of it. First, I think that Congress obviously has a role to play in that. I think there has to be broad buy-in politically for this agreement to succeed in the long term, because of course Congress will have a role in lifting sanctions. The next administration, whatever it is, will have a role in upholding this agreement. So I think you need to have that broad political buy-in and that is very important.

Look, I do think that from where we are now we should be focused on those principles which Dr. Heinonen articulated and making sure that whatever agreement comes out is as strong as possible. But I do think that we should consider that any final sanctions relief again be dependent not just on these particular steps, but on evidence of that broader strategic shift by Iran, evidence that Iran is in fact going in a different direction, and therefore there is perhaps more trust, more confidence that they will actually uphold their side of the bargain.

Then frankly, again, we can take steps on the other side, because for a state to agree to a deal is not just about what is in the deal. It is about what is the alternative, and we need to make steps to make that alternative look worse from Iran's perspective. I think that means strengthening the credibility of the sanctions threat, strengthening the credibility of the military threat. I think if we do those things, then perhaps we can influence Iran's perception of what is a good deal.

Senator CORKER. Thank you both. I know it is a lot of trouble to prepare testimony and be here. We all benefit greatly from it and I want to thank you both for being here. Typically, about noon at these hearings things kind of clear out to other meetings, but I know people are paying attention and have read your written testimony. So thank you.

The CHAIRMAN. Well, thank you, Senator Corker. Sometimes our second panels, with all due respect to the first panel, is as important, if not more insightful.

So let me ask you one final set of questions. I want to revisit, Dr. Heinonen, something you responded to Senator Corker which to me is not insignificant. Basically, you said when the Iranian Ambassador, among their complaints to the IAEA, was complaining about the way in which the IAEA was issuing its reports to its member states, that the reason that it is important for the IAEA to issue its report to its member states in the manner in which they are doing is because then member states can use their own intelligence and information to judge whether what the IAEA has been told is along the lines of what they know from their intelligence or is deviating significantly from it, in which case in this case Iran, if that were the case, would not be coming clean.

Is that what I am hearing you say?

Dr. HEINONEN. Yes, this is one thing, certainly. The other thing is that the member states can then do their own independent judgment how well Iran complies with the requirements of, let us say, the P5+1 agreement.

The CHAIRMAN. So it is not insignificant when the Iranian Ambassador says, I do not like the way, I do not agree, I think you are not reporting correctly. It may look like an insignificant element, but it can be very significant if member states are going to make a judgment whether there is a forthcoming Iran in this respect.

Dr. HEINONEN. Yes. This complaint has been there about the last 5 years from the Iranians. It started to arise somewhere around 2007, 2006. So it has been quite some time there. It is repeated, repeated. I personally thought that with this new team there in Teheran that this kind of language disappears, but apparently it is not the case.

The CHAIRMAN. Mr. Singh, one final set of questions. You argued that during the interim agreement the United States made concessions to Iran, including on uranium enrichment. What other concessions do you feel were made? How do you judge what Iran did in response under the agreement? How do you judge the concessions, what you define as concessions, versus what Iran did?

You also, in response to Senator Corker, said we need to strengthen our sanctions regime, our military threat. What are examples of what you would suggest would do that?

Mr. SINGH. Sure. On your first question, look, I think the whole underlying dynamic of the negotiations has changed in a fundamental way. When we were crafting U.N. Security Council resolutions in the 2000s and we got a number of unanimous U.N. Security Council resolutions, the point was to address these Iranian violations of its international obligations and put the burden on Iran to demonstrate its peaceful intent.

I do feel as though now that narrative, that underlying framework, has shifted to this question of providing Iran's practical needs or satisfying its purported rights in a way that is safe and monitored and so forth. That is a very important shift. One of the things that Iran has tried to do in addition to its effort to undermine the credibility of the IAEA is to show that it stood up to the U.N. Security Council, whose legitimacy it has also impugned.

So that in itself, that change in the dynamic, is an important change in itself. When it comes to the particulars, I think we made that vital concession on Iran enriching indefinitely, which is something that Iran has been seeking since literally the inception of these talks in 2003. We conceded that any constraints that Iran is under will be temporary in nature and perhaps quite short, in fact, in nature, and so that Iran will be treated like any other state at the end of this process, despite again those obligations.

We have granted some implicit legitimacy to those facilities, which, remember, were constructed in secret and in violation of its NPT obligations. That includes Natanz, Fordow, Arak, and some other facilities, which now will remain in place and not be dismantled, I believe.

We have not forced Iran to address the weaponization question or the ballistic missile question. So I think all of these things are significant concessions that we have made in the course of these talks.

On the second part—how do we bolster the credibility of the ''or else,'' as it were. Look, I do think it is important that there be a clear message to Iran about what are the consequences for not reaching a decent agreement by the end of these talks. I think that should be a unified message. Here is an issue where I think there is strong bipartisan agreement in the United States and the messages we are sending should reflect that strong bipartisan agreement.

I do think it is very important that we continue to enforce vigorously the sanctions which are already in place, that have not been suspended as part of the JPOA. I am concerned, for example, by reports that China's oil imports from Iran have increased 48 percent if you look at the first 6 months of 2014 compared to the first 6 months of 2013. And yet there has not been as far as I can tell an appreciable response.

Now, part of that is condensates, but I am not sure why that should be important to a U.S. policymaker because that strikes me as a technical loophole in sanctions that could be corrected.

When it comes to the military credibility, I think, look, that is harder, because I think we have implanted in the minds of folks around the world the idea that we are a lot less inclined to address situations like those in Syria, in Iraq, and elsewhere in a sort of forceful way. We did not enforce the red line in Syria. We have not done much of anything, frankly, in Syria to uphold our stated policy. We have responded in similar ways to Iraq. When it comes to Ukraine, for example, I think our response has been relatively modest compared to what is actually happening there.

So part of the answer is addressing some of these situations around the world in a more purposeful and a more decisive way. I think we need to stress our continuing commitment to this region. I think the messaging often that we send out is that, well, we are pivoting to a different region, we may not have much of an interest in this region anymore because of energy independence and things like that. I think it is important that we get that message straight.

Then again, since especially 2011 I think some of our alliances in the region have suffered and I think we need to again rebuild that security architecture which we once enjoyed in the region.

So I think there are a number of steps on either side of the ledger when it comes to reenforcing that credibility. But again, without that "or else" I do not see why Iran would be motivated to accept a deal which places restrictions on its activities.

The CHAIRMAN. I would note that the one thing that is very clear to me is that military assets that did not exist or were not in position in the region are placed in the region, which should send the Iranians a very clear message that if in fact we cannot strike a deal and if sanctions, ratcheted up sanctions, do not get them to rethink a break in negotiations if that is what happens, that there is a real credible threat, because those assets were not in the region prior to this process, they are in the region now, and I would hope that that would be some sense of messaging to them.

Well, look. With the thanks of the committee for your expertise, and I hope we can continue to call upon you, the record will remain open until the close of business tomorrow. With the thanks of the committee, this hearing is adjourned.

[Whereupon, at 12:43 p.m., the hearing was adjourned.]

ADDITIONAL MATERIAL SUBMITTED FOR THE RECORD

RESPONSES OF WENDY SHERMAN TO QUESTIONS SUBMITTED BY SENATOR BOB CORKER

Question. During the hearing you argued: "if you are asking . . . whether we are going to come to Congress for legislative action to affirm a comprehensive agreement, we believe, as other administrations do, that the executive branch has the authority to take such executive action on this kind of a political understanding that might be reached with Iran."

- What kind of "political understanding" are we seeking from Iran (please cite the previous types of political understandings you have in mind here)? Will this be a treaty? A congressional-executive agreement? An executive agreement? If an executive agreement, how and why does it fall short of an arms control treaty or congressional-executive agreement?

Answer. The Senate has a constitutional role in giving its advice and consent to the ratification of treaties, which are legally binding international agreements. All the States participating in the negotiations on a comprehensive solution with Iran have taken the position that the resulting document would not impose international legal obligations. This intent will be carefully reflected in the drafting of the document. It is not uncommon for states to conclude that a nonlegally binding arrangement would best promote their objectives (for example, the Helsinki Final Act, the Proliferation Security Initiative, the Nuclear Suppliers Group, and the Missile Technology Control Regime).

If Iran fails to live up to its commitments, the United States and our allies will have the flexibility to reimpose sanctions, both under the terms of a comprehensive solution and as a matter of U.S. law. Even though the comprehensive solution would be neither a treaty nor an executive agreement, Congress of course has an important role in U.S. foreign policy, and we will continue to keep Congress closely apprised of our progress in these negotiations.

The views of the Congress are significantly informing our approach to these negotiations. Building the sanctions regime was a major achievement in which Congress played a leading role, and if negotiations are successful, the administration will work with Congress to develop an appropriate mechanism for long-term sanctions relief.

However, any measure calling for a vote by Congress on a potential comprehensive deal between the P5+1 and Iran risks dividing the United States and our P5+1 partners and undermining our position vis-a-vis Iran by signaling that U.S. negotiators are not empowered to make decisions and sowing doubt about U.S. intentions. Congress now has a responsibility to facilitate a successful conclusion of the negotiations by giving the President and our partners the space needed to pursue negotiations.

Question. Is it the position of the administration that the spread of enrichment and reprocessing should be halted? How does an agreement that allows Iran to enrich uranium impact the administration's ability to achieve gold standard civil nuclear cooperation agreements across the Middle East? Throughout other regions? Do we lose our moral ground in asking nations to forgo enrichment and reprocessing when we acknowledge Iran—globally recognized as a poor actor—as an enricher?

Answer. The Obama administration has continued to uphold and promote longstanding U.S. policy opposing the spread of enrichment and reprocessing (ENR) technologies. The United States employs a range of measures, both multilateral and bilateral, to help minimize the spread of ENR technologies around the world.

As for Iran, in line with the Obama administration's policy opposing the spread of ENR technologies, the JPOA has halted the progress of Iran's nuclear program and rolled it back in key respects, including by committing Iran to limit its enrichment capacity and to dilute or fabricate into fuel its stockpile of near-20-percent low enriched uranium. The JPOA specifies that a comprehensive solution would involve a "mutually defined enrichment programme with practical limits and transparency measures to ensure the peaceful nature of the programme." While we believe Iran's fuel needs could and should be met by the international market, we are prepared to consider in the end state a strictly limited enrichment program consistent with Iran's practical needs, but only if the Iranians accept rigorous limits on, and transparent monitoring of, the scope and level of enrichment activities, capacity—where it is carried out—and stocks of enriched uranium.

If we can reach an understanding with Iran on strict constraints, then we can contemplate an arrangement that includes a very modest amount of enrichment while also constraining Iran's capacity to obtain a nuclear weapon. Such an outcome is preferable to the alternative; a program that is unconstrained and less monitored that could be used to produce material for nuclear weapons. It should also be noted that, with respect to reprocessing, the JPOA halts further progress on the reactor at Arak and provides that Iran will not engage in reprocessing or construction of a facility capable of reprocessing, and it further states that a comprehensive solution would continue this prohibition and "fully resolve the concerns related to the reactor at Arak."

More broadly, we will continue our efforts to prevent the spread of ENR technologies, making use of the various tools at our disposal to achieve our nonproliferation goals. As part of this effort, we seek to ensure that states make the choice to rely on the international market for fuel cycle services. If we are not sufficiently convinced that potential nuclear cooperation with a particular country would be consistent with our policy goals on ENR, we would not conclude a 123 Agreement with that country.

Question. In October 2013 you testified that "we don't have a lot of time [to negotiate]." Now you've put more time on the clock. Will you commit that this will be the one and only extension of the interim deal?

Answer. We extended the Joint Plan of Action until November 24, 2014, which is 1 year from the date we concluded the Joint Plan of Action in Geneva. The Joint Plan of Action references the year timeframe for negotiating a comprehensive agreement, stating: "The final step of a comprehensive solution, which the parties aim to conclude negotiating and commence implementing no more than one year after the adoption of this document . . ."

We decided to extend these negotiations because we have made progress and we see a path forward, although we have more work to do on many key issues. We are focused on doing everything we can to reach a comprehensive solution that assures the international community that Iran's program is for exclusively peaceful purposes.

Question. Is it still the administration's requirement that (in your own words) Iran "come clean on its past actions as part of any comprehensive agreement" and completely resolve any and all concerns about the Iranian nuclear program's military dimensions?

Answer. Resolution of our concerns about the possible military dimensions (PMD) of Iran's nuclear program is an important part of a comprehensive deal. Our position is that Iran must fully cooperate with the International Atomic Energy Agency (IAEA), including by providing access to facilities, individuals, documents, and information requested by the IAEA. Our approach to timing and sequencing of sanctions relief for a comprehensive deal makes clear that Iran will not get the sanctions relief it seeks until PMD issues are resolved to the satisfaction of the IAEA.

We will not reach any final deal unless and until we are satisfied that there can be no further military dimension to Iran's nuclear program and that any past efforts to develop a nuclear warhead are permanently discontinued.

Question. Has Iran complied with all elements of the Joint Plan of Action and its associated implementation guidelines? Iran has exceeded the 1 million barrel per day crude export limits for every month of the JPOA, averaging roughly 1.3 million barrels per day over the first 6 months of 2014 and currently at 1.4 million barrels per day. Explain in detail how they have complied with this requirement using your official estimates.

Answer. Since the Joint Plan of Action (JPOA) went into effect on January 20, 2014, we have continuously tracked data on Iran's crude oil exports to evaluate Iran's adherence to its JPOA commitments. We now have data covering almost the entire JPOA period. The data suggest that our efforts were successful. From January 20 through June, Iran's average daily crude oil export volumes remained at the level that existed when the JPOA came into force: 1–1.1 million barrels per day. This is a testament to the unity of purpose the international community has displayed in encouraging Iran to work with us and our allies on a comprehensive solution to its nuclear program. We have also maintained engagement at the highest level with all six of Iran's current purchasers of crude oil, urging them to continue abiding by our JPOA understanding on their levels of crude oil imports.

It should be noted that some reports of Iran's "crude oil" export volumes include not only crude oil but also other hydrocarbon liquids, such as condensate. These reports thus make Iran's crude oil export volumes appear larger than they actually are. In accordance with congressional legislation, these other hydrocarbon liquids are not covered by the JPOA.

Furthermore, Iran's reported crude oil export volumes often include shipments to Syria. We are indeed concerned about Iran's crude oil deliveries to Syria, but not in the context of JPOA compliance since Syria is not a paying customer. Since Syria does not pay, it does not meaningfully contribute to Iran's economy, which in turn means that shipments to Syria do not relax the pressure on Iran during the negotiations. I assure you however, that we are closely following the crude deliveries to Syria and addressing it.

Final data for July are still outstanding, but once that is in I would be happy to arrange a classified briefing that reflects information for the complete JPOA period. We do not expect it to have a material effect on the overall volumes.

RESPONSES OF DAVID S. COHEN TO QUESTIONS
SUBMITTED BY SENATOR BOB CORKER

Question. A recent study by the Washington Institute for Near East Policy argued Iran used the "time and space" provided by the JPOA to stabilize its economy, leading to a decrease in inflation from over 40 percent in early 2013 to 17 percent today, and projecting 1.5 percent GDP growth this year and 2.3 percent per year thereafter, even if they do not get further sanctions relief.

- ◆ What is your assessment of this report and these macroeconomic indicators? Do you dispute the overall trajectory of the Iranian economy?

Answer. The Iranian economy remains under enormous economic pressure. For the year ending in March 2013, Iran's real GDP contracted by almost 7 percent, pushing Iran's economy into a deep recession. Iran's economy then contracted a further 2 percent through March 2014. Whatever growth Iran may achieve is over a significantly smaller base. Although year-over-year inflation is around the levels WINEP estimates, Iran's average annual inflation remains one of the highest rates in the world.

These metrics, moreover, must be considered against the backdrop of Iran's ongoing economic disorder. In 2014 our oil sanctions alone deprived Iran of over $40 billion in oil revenue—well over twice the total estimated $14–15 billion value of the JPOA, and since 2012 it has foregone or been denied full access to more than $200 billion in oil revenues. It will forgo another $15 billion over the course of the latest JPOA period from lost oil sales. Moreover, as a result of the recent decline in oil prices—which Iranian officials have described as a "new sanction"—the government has said it is considering a budget based on a price of $40/barrel of oil, as opposed to $100/barrel the previous year. In addition, the vast majority of Iran's approximately $100 billion in foreign exchange holdings, including revenues from oil sales, are largely inaccessible or restricted by sanctions. The Iranian rial, moreover, has depreciated by around 56 percent since November 2013 when the JPOA was concluded. The limited, temporary, and reversible sanctions relief provided for under the JPOA has by no means alleviated the Iranian economy's fundamental weaknesses.

It is true that since the election of President Rouhani in June 2013, there has been some improvement in a few economic indicators. President Rouhani, in stark contrast to his predecessor, has taken policy measures to stabilize the economy that have contributed to improving economic performance. That improvement, however, is largely independent of and cannot be solely attributed to the limited sanctions relief in the JPOA. For Iran to have any hope of realizing meaningful, sustainable economic progress, it needs more significant sanctions relief, and that can only be achieved if Iran can assure the international community that its nuclear program is, and will remain, exclusively peaceful.

Question. What is your estimate of the effects on Iran's economy of the sanctions relief likely to be provided in any final nuclear deal? Will sanctions relief include Iranian access to SWIFT?

Answer. If Iran commits to undertake the steps necessary to assure the international community that its nuclear program is and will remain exclusively peaceful, it can expect to see significant sanctions relief, potentially including increased access to the international financial system. The JPOA provides that a comprehensive solution regarding Iran's nuclear program would include the lifting of our domestic, nuclear-related sanctions, in addition to U.N. Security Council sanctions. The effects on Iran's economy will depend on the precise contours of the relief, which are core subjects of our ongoing negotiations with Iran. Any such relief would depend on Iran taking specific nuclear steps and our confidence that Iran is living up to its commitments. However, U.S. sanctions dealing with Iran's support for terrorist groups such as Hamas and Hezbollah and its human rights abuses will remain in place.

Question. In the event of Iranian noncompliance with a comprehensive agreement, how will relief be structured in such a way to punish Iran for such a violation?

Answer. The sanctions relief that would be provided in any comprehensive solution will depend on Iran's continued compliance with its own commitments. We will take action as appropriate in the event Iran fails to abide by its commitments. The United States and the EU will be in a position to reimpose sanctions promptly, and we are seeking to structure UNSC sanctions relief to ensure that those sanctions will snap back into place in the event that Iran does not meet its commitments.

––––––––

RESPONSES OF WENDY SHERMAN TO QUESTIONS
SUBMITTED BY SENATOR MARCO RUBIO

Question. Has there been any progress made during your multiple discussions with Iranian officials in obtaining the releases of Americans imprisoned or missing in Iran such as Pastor Saeed Abedini, Robert Levinson, or Amir Hekmati?

Answer. The U.S. Government is dedicated to the return of Robert Levinson, and dual U.S. citizens Saeed Abedini, Amir Hekmati. We also call on Iran to release U.S.-Iranian citizen, Jason Rezaian, and the others who were detained with him.

The President, the Secretary, and I have raised the cases of Mr. Levinson, Mr. Hekmati, and Mr. Abedini directly with the Iranian Government. We have made clear that we are calling on Iran to release Mr. Hekmati and Mr. Abedini, and to work cooperatively with us to locate Mr. Levinson, so they can be reunited with their families.

At our request, the Swiss Government, in its role as our protecting power, has also continued to raise the issue on our behalf, as have other countries that we have asked to press Iran to cooperate on these cases.

We will continue to pursue all available options until all three Americans return home safely.

Question. Will any of these issues—support for terrorism, human rights, or captive American citizens, be addressed as part of any final agreement with Iran?

Answer. Discussions through the P5+1 have focused exclusively on the nuclear issue. However, even as we negotiate with Iran over its nuclear program, we continue to take issue with Iran's human rights abuses, state sponsorship of terrorism, its detainment of U.S. citizens, and its destabilizing activities across the region. We will not ignore this behavior even if we are able to reach a nuclear deal with Iran.

Question. Have you made clear to your Iranian interlocutors that it is Congress and a future administration that will make decisions about long-term sanctions relief and not the current administration?

Answer. It is still too early to determine what an exact sanctions relief package would look like, but comprehensive sanctions relief would require a mix of executive and legislative actions. Iran is aware of that dynamic. Iran is also aware that we are seeking a long-term comprehensive agreement. Under that agreement, sanctions relief would come only after Iran has taken certain steps, as verified by the International Atomic Energy Agency (IAEA). We do not believe that our concerns would be resolved at the start of implementation of a comprehensive deal, as it will likely take Iran time to complete the many steps it will have to take.

Question. Have you indicated to them that U.S.-Iranian relations will not substantially change until progress is made in these nonnuclear areas?

Answer. Iran is aware of our deep and serious concerns with its activities. It understands that a comprehensive agreement over its nuclear program—if possible—will not detract us from taking issue with a great deal of its behavior, including its human rights abuses, state sponsorship of terrorism, detention of U.S. citizens, and destabilizing role in the region. We will not ignore this behavior even if we reach a nuclear deal, and we will not hesitate to put pressure on Iran when it is warranted.

RESPONSES OF DAVID S. COHEN TO QUESTIONS
SUBMITTED BY SENATOR MARCO RUBIO

Question. Can you confirm that Chinese oil imports from Iran were 48 percent above the 2013 levels? What level of Chinese imports would result in imposition of sanctions?

Answer. Public reports of China's purchases of Iranian crude oil must be carefully interpreted. For instance, reports of China's "oil imports" often include not only crude oil but also other hydrocarbon liquids and petroleum products. These reports can thus make China's purchases of Iranian crude oil appear larger than they actually are. The Joint Plan of Action (JPOA) between P5+1 and Iran only applies to purchase levels of crude oil from Iran by current customers, including China.

It is also important to distinguish fluctuations in China's (or any other country's) purchases of Iranian crude oil—due to seasonality, delivery schedules, weather, and other factors—from the trend in those purchases over the full JPOA period. For example, while public reports indicate that China's April purchases were above trend, the same reports indicate that China's August purchases were significantly below trend. Bearing these month-to-month fluctuations in mind, we continue to closely monitor China's imports, as well as those of Iran's five other oil customers, over the remainder of the JPOA period.

Question. Iranian oil exports overall stand at 1.4 million barrels per day, 40 percent higher than the limit envisaged in the JPOA. What does this Iranian violation of the JPOA's terms say about their willingness to abide by the requirements of a future agreement?

Answer. Since implementation of the Joint Plan of Action (JPOA) began on January 20, 2014, we have continuously tracked data on Iran's crude oil exports in light of the provision in the JPOA that such exports remain at pre-JPOA levels. The data suggest that our efforts have been successful. Throughout the JPOA to date, Iran's average daily crude oil export volumes remained at the level that existed when implementation of the JPOA began: 1–1.1 million barrels per day. This is a testament to the unity of purpose the international community has displayed in encouraging Iran to work with us and our allies on a comprehensive solution to its nuclear program. We have also maintained engagement at the highest level with all six of Iran's current purchasers of crude oil (i.e., China, India, Japan, South Korea, Turkey, and Taiwan), urging them to continue importing Iranian crude oil at the levels that were in existence when implementation of the JPOA began.

It should be noted that some public reports of Iran's "oil export" volumes include not only crude oil but also other hydrocarbon liquids and petroleum products. These reports can thus make Iran's crude oil export volumes appear larger than they actually are. The JPOA only applies to purchase levels of crude oil from Iran by current customers.

Furthermore, Iran's reported crude oil export volumes often include shipments to Syria. We are indeed concerned about Iran's crude oil deliveries to Syria. Since Syria is not a paying customer, however, these shipments do not meaningfully contribute to Iran's economy, which, in turn, alleviates concerns that these shipments to Syria relax the pressure on Iran during the negotiations.

We would be happy to discuss these and other issues in more detail in an appropriate setting.

———

RESPONSE OF WENDY SHERMAN TO QUESTION
SUBMITTED BY SENATOR JEFF FLAKE

Question. Any deal reached with Iran would be of historic magnitude, and of great importance to the United States as well as the rest of the world. Such matters have in the past been negotiated through treaties, a recent example of which is the New START agreement with Russia. Treaties require approval by the Senate. However, the administration has negotiated other matters of great importance such as the Strategic Partnership Agreement with Afghanistan without consultation of Congress.

◆ How has the administration determined what international matters of great importance will be subjected to approval by the Senate, and which ones will not?

◆ Will any final deal with Iran be subject to approval of the Senate on the merits of the deal itself?

◆ Do you believe the Senate should weigh in on any final agreement?

Answer. The Senate has a constitutional role in giving its advice and consent to the ratification of treaties, which are legally binding international agreements. All the States participating in the negotiations on a comprehensive solution with Iran have taken the position that the resulting document would not impose international legal obligations. This intent will be carefully reflected in the drafting of the document. It is not uncommon for states to conclude that a nonlegally binding arrangement would best promote their objectives (for example, the Helsinki Final Act, the Proliferation Security Initiative, the Nuclear Suppliers Group, and the Missile Technology Control Regime).

If Iran fails to live up to its commitments, the United States and our allies will have the flexibility to reimpose sanctions, both under the terms of a comprehensive solution and as a matter of U.S. law. Even though the comprehensive solution would be neither a treaty nor an Executive agreement, Congress of course has an important role in U.S. foreign policy, and we will continue to keep Congress closely apprised of our progress in these negotiations.

The views of the Congress are significantly informing our approach to these negotiations. Building the sanctions regime was a major achievement in which Congress played a leading role, and if negotiations are successful, the administration will work with Congress to develop an appropriate mechanism for long-term sanctions relief.

However, any measure calling for a vote by Congress on a potential comprehensive deal between the P5+1 and Iran risks dividing the United States and our P5+1 partners and undermining our position vis-a-vis Iran by signaling that U.S. negotiators are not empowered to make decisions and sowing doubt about U.S. intentions. Congress now has a responsibility to facilitate a successful conclusion of the negotiations by giving the President and our partners the space needed to pursue negotiations.